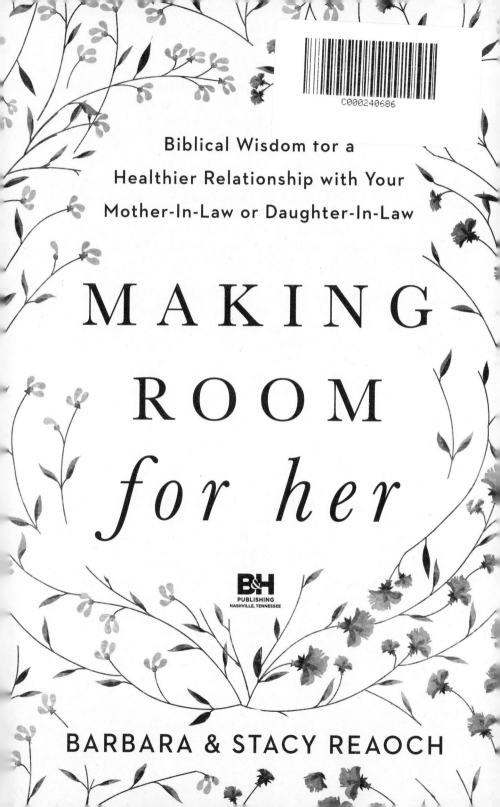

Biblical Wisdom for a
Healthier Relationship with Your
Mother-In-Law or Daughter-In-Law

MAKING
ROOM
for her

B&H
PUBLISHING
NASHVILLE, TENNESSEE

BARBARA & STACY REAOCH

978-1-0877-4638-8

Published by B&H Publishing Group
Nashville, Tennessee

Dewey Decimal Classification: 306.87
Subject Heading: MOTHERS-IN-LAW / DAUGHTERS-IN-LAW /
DOMESTIC RELATIONS

Cover design by Lindy Martin, FaceOut. Cover images by cristatus/
shutterstock and JOJOSTUDIO/shutterstock. Photo of Barbara
Reaoch by Chad Swanson Photography. Photo of Stacy Reaoch by
Brittian Flatt Photography.

1 2 3 4 5 6 • 26 25 24 23 22

To the women of Three Rivers Grace Church and our friends who prayed and shared their stories. Your transparency helped us understand the struggles and hope in the mother-in-law/daughter-in-law relationship. Through you we saw that making room for "her" is possible by God's grace.

—Barbara and Stacy

ACKNOWLEDGMENTS

The words in this book were a group project. We are indebted to the many women who shared their stories with us. Their transparency in telling us their experiences set the stage for this book.

From Barb:

A great thank you to the men and women in our small group who, for many months, lovingly prayed and asked, "How's the book going?" This book benefited, in untold ways, from friends who read and reread each chapter. How I appreciate the keen insights and editing skills of my faithful friends—Deb Deal, Janet Rentsch, Neatice Warner, and Shirley Mills. Endless thanks to Sara Brigman for using your gifts and Godward focus to consistently point me to a gospel-centered message.

From Stacy:

To the women of Three Rivers Grace Church, thank you for your excitement, support, and prayers for this endeavor. Jen Hovis, Faith Walker, and Rachel Clayton, thank you for holding up my arms when my strength was weary (and for swooping in when I needed a dose of encouragement, chocolate, and chai tea lattes!). To Lindsey Carlson, Jen Oshman, and Irene Sun, what a precious gift to have fellow sisters in ministry and writing comrades. Thank you for taking the time to read early versions of the manuscript and offer feedback, even in the midst of your own writing projects.

Mega thanks to our B&H acquisitions editor Ashley Gorman. God has gifted you with wisdom beyond your years. Your expertise touches every page of this book.

To Don Gates, thank you for championing this book and helping us navigate the publishing world.

We feel tremendously blessed to be part of the B&H family and are grateful for the fantastic marketing team and our specialist, Stacey Sapp, for all they do to get books into the hands of women.

To Milaina, Noah, Annalyse, and Micah, thank you for the excitement over your mom and Ouma's book. You are precious treasures. Milaina, thank you for always being interested in what we're writing and asking about details that no one else does. To Kim, Elizabeth, and Carol, thank you for reading drafts and giving insights in a way that only sisters and daughters can.

To Ron, thank you for being our steadfast support. In all things, in all ways, your grace-filled love and leadership gives perspective and joy to our family.

And to the man who brought these two women together in relationship, Ben. Thank you for your constant support, your loving encouragement, and your editing expertise. Thank you for late night talks and running to our aid when we had tech issues (again). We are so grateful for your patient spirit and the steadfast pillar of strength you are in our family and church.

And especially a thank you to God. You are our Rock. This pandemic year reminded us that life is but a vapor. Our prayer is that You alone are magnified and glorified, in our lives and writing.

CONTENTS

INTRODUCTION

A re you ready to cultivate a healthier in-law relationship? Or maybe you're ready to give up, wondering if your hard relationship is hopeless. The truth is, even in the best of times, family relationships can challenge us. God puts us in families to give us a place where we can be nurtured and secure. But families also disappoint us and tempt us to bitterness. Whether you are opening this book with an expectant heart or as a last resort, we pray you'll find hope and help.

Our names are Barbara and Stacy Reaoch, and we are not experts on the mother-in-law/daughter-in-law relationship. We are merely two women whose hearts God has graciously joined together through the life of one man—Stacy's husband and Barb's son! We're here to tell our story and give you hope. With twenty years of ups and downs, we've known some hard times. But God has been at work. No matter how we may have messed up, God has always shown up to help us—to grow our love and appreciation for one another. Even though we are women from different backgrounds, with different personalities and diverse priorities, we've found common ground; more than that, genuine love. Perhaps you wonder if God could do the same for you. By letting you in on our struggles and triumphs and hard-won lessons learned, we're here to say this: *he can*.

We haven't written a book of coping strategies. Nor are these pages filled solely with personal advice (though we chime

in with practical ideas from time to time). We don't ignore difficult issues and tell you to simply hope for the best. Instead,
we ask hard questions: Why are in-law relationships so challenging? Why do in-law dynamics break down? Why is it so easy to
offend or be offended and so hard to forgive? As we explore
these things together, our ultimate aim is to point you to the
only One who gives lasting transforming truth—Jesus! As he
has helped us in his Word and through his Spirit, Jesus will
meet your deepest need in your in-law relationship.

Every relationship—even the in-law-relationship—is a can-
vas on which the Master Artist paints the glorious truth of the
gospel. With every phone call or family gathering, God paints
another stroke. He is always working. He is faithful to his promise to use all things for our good. Out of the ordinary, even with
her, he is creating beauty.

We don't know what your relationship is like with "her,"
your in-law. Perhaps it's in a decent place. Or perhaps you've
been hurt. Maybe you fear the risk of another heart-breaking
failure, even in picking up this book. Find comfort in this: as
we developed each chapter, we talked with many women. And
we heard the hurt and hesitation in their hearts. Some had to
come to grips with the hard truth that not every relationship
ends happily on this earth. Others learned that even when
they did not understand God's purposes, that they could trust
him. Still others have seen God work wonders in their in-law
relationship as they've intentionally put his Word into practice.
While all of their stories are different, and the status of their
relationships with "her" are in varying places on the spectrum
of enjoyment, one thing is true for them all: God moved inside
them. And isn't that the real miracle? That God changes your
relationship with *her* by changing *you*?

One of us took the lead in writing each chapter, but as a whole, the book weaves together our mutual input. The book is written from the perspective of two believers, given that both of us know the Lord, but as we go, we also include words to the woman whose in-law is not a believer.

As we wrote, we waded through several hard conversations. Open discussion drew us closer together in surprising new ways, deepening our love for each other. Given how much that discussion helped us in writing the book, we pray that you will read it in conversation with other women so that you, too, might benefit from the power of communal processing. To aid you in this, each chapter ends with questions that are designed to start a conversation between you and God, you and your in-law, and if you are in a small group, with other women.

Jesus is all about hope. He sees those who are hurting. His heart of compassion always acts to help. He comforts us through his Spirit and his Word. We pray you see Jesus on every page. As you read, ask God to open your eyes, to see his heart, and to make you more like his Son as you navigate your in-law relationship. He gives hope that never disappoints. ✒

> This hope will not disappoint us, because God's love has been poured out in our hearts through the Holy Spirit who was given to us. (Rom. 5:5)

FIRST IMPRESSIONS

How Our Past Shapes the Present

W ould any of you being willing to talk with me about your relationship with your mother-in-law?" Stacy asked a group of women she had dinner with. Immediately there were groans mixed with nervous laughs. "How much time do you have?" said one of them. "Can this be anonymous?"

It's no surprise that talking about this relationship can be a touchy subject. From the intrusive mother-in-law on the TV show *Everybody Loves Raymond* to jokes cracked among a group of moms enjoying a night out together, there's a common thread of the dreaded mother-in-law.

How often are our impressions shaped by the stereotypes around us? On *Everybody Loves Raymond*, Marie Barone and her husband, Frank, live next door to their adult son, Raymond, and his wife, Debra. Marie constantly shows up at the house, unannounced, critiquing Debra's housekeeping and cooking skills. "Maybe the children would like to try something homemade for a change?" she says as Debra stirs the box macaroni and cheese.

Debra manages to put on a good face for Marie, but then explodes behind closed doors to her husband, frustrated with her mother-in-law's constant intrusions. The tension between the women even makes Debra want to hide the fact that her family is at home in order to avoid more interactions with her mother-in-law (which we'll shorten to MIL as we go). The in-law relationship provides sitcoms with lots of material. Many situations are extreme, but the producers and directors know that women identify with just how strained this relationship can be.

Barbara asked a similar question to other women, "How would you describe your relationship with your daughter-in-law?" Diane spoke of the disappointment in realizing that she and her daughter-in-law (which we'll shorten to DIL as we go) "are not quite family and will never really be friends." Stephanie recounted how her DIL leaves strict instructions of how to care for her three-year-old. "It makes me feel like my DIL doesn't trust my judgment. She must think I didn't do a very good job raising her husband." With every visit, Marilyn says, "I've learned to bite my tongue around my DIL. I know she's insecure in her new role, but she often finds fault with what I say. My son hears about it the minute I leave."

In real life, we're not as likely to laugh at our strained relationships. The frustration can lead us to pull away or isolate ourselves, avoiding the in-law that makes us feel like we're not good enough. The cultural stereotypes of in-laws being difficult can make us prone to expect the worst. We might go into our marriage with low expectations of the in-law relationship because of what we saw happen in our parents' lives, or what we see on TV. Our first impression might be a negative one that sets us up for a disappointing relationship from the get-go.

≁

Kate knew that her boyfriend's relationship with his mom was strained. The first time she went to meet her, Brandon refused to take her to the home he grew up in. Instead he wanted to find a neutral place, a baseball game, that wouldn't be flooded with the painful memories he had of growing up. Kate had a positive outlook on the relationship. Sure, Brandon had a difficult childhood and a strained relationship with his parents. But Kate thought this would be an opportunity to win her future MIL over. *I can help smooth things over,* she thought to herself.

Little did she know just how difficult that would prove to be.

The first meeting with her MIL was less than ideal. While she expected that Brandon's mom would ask her questions to get to know her, she seemed completely uninterested in engaging in conversation. Instead, she wildly cheered for the baseball team, fixing her full attention on the game. Kate repeatedly tried to ask her questions throughout the game, but felt surprised and hurt that it wasn't reciprocated. That initial rocky start gave a bleak outlook for the future. Suddenly the dream of having a close-knit relationship with her MIL was clouded by the fear of future negative interactions.

Sue felt certain that she and her future DIL would enjoy a better-than-typical relationship. In her desire to be a loving MIL, Sue read all she could about her new role. She decided to "think before speaking" to avoid words that might lead to a misunderstanding. Knowing her rigid tendencies, Sue asked God for help! Flexibility—an openness to new ideas and experiences—would make her more approachable.

Everyone wanted a dream-come-true wedding for the young couple. A lengthy invitation list, and high-end reception venue created a financial strain. At the couple's request, Sue and her husband decided to share the wedding expenses. But how should they respond when the bride's less-than-wise decisions meant greater costs? Sue and her husband decided to overlook their disappointment. Yet more unwise decisions made it harder to ignore their future DIL's self-interest. Was Sue overly sensitive? She wondered. But then her husband asked why the bride-to-be ignored or rejected many of Sue's loving attempts of support. Negative interactions dampened Sue's hope for that better-than-typical relationship she once hoped for.

The Root of Our Problem

No matter what kind of difficult relationship you might have—whether it be mother-in-law and daughter-in-law, parent to child, or employer and employee—we all have the same basic issue. Romans 3:23 says "for all have all sinned and fall short of the glory of God." We are selfish creatures who instinctively put our own needs and desires first. We create our ideal schedule and fit people in around our activities. We think about what works best for me and how I can look good in the situation. What is the easiest and most comfortable situation for myself?

Without the grace of God, we rely on our own faulty self-will to do the right thing. But our hope is found in the gospel. If you have turned away from sin and cried out to the Lord and his work on the cross for forgiveness, you can be sure that his Holy Spirit indwells you. And the Holy Spirit allows us to draw on the grace and power of God to change us from the inside out.

Second Corinthians 5:17 tells us that "if anyone is in Christ, he is a new creation; the old has passed away, and see, the new has come!" We've been given the mind of Christ and can pray that as we grow in our faith, the fruit of the Spirit will abound in our lives—love, joy, peace, patience, kindness, goodness, faithfulness, gentleness, and self-control (Gal. 5:22–23). There is no relationship that is without hope. The mother-in-law/ daughter-in-law relationship is complex. But when the power of God is involved, we can trust that change and growth are possible.

We know that every MIL/DIL relationship is different. But it might be helpful for you, as you read our words in this book, to understand our first impressions of one another.

Stacy's First Impression

I first met my mother-in-law when I was barely seventeen years old. Ben Reaoch and I were introduced by mutual friends at the county fair. We struck up a friendship (or rather, I got to know him in hopes of a Homecoming date) and we soon began spending time together. I remember the first time I walked into his beautiful home. Barbara was sitting on the couch, Bible in her lap, with a huge smile to greet me. She was warm and friendly and instantly made me feel welcome. But there was something different about Ben's family.

Ben's house was filled with Christian books, Bibles, commentaries and even a list of things to pray for on the kitchen table. *That seems strange*, I thought to myself. My view of prayer was something that happened in church or before a holiday meal. Even though I considered myself a Christian, I didn't attend church regularly. My Bible sat on my bookshelf as a trophy from confirmation class. But it became obvious that the Bible was a well-loved book in Ben's house. Little did I realize that Barbara's warm smile and hospitable spirit was a fruit of God working in her life.

As Ben and I got to know each other, I enjoyed spending time at his house. I was well aware that Ben's family was much more religious than my own. But it didn't stop me from wanting to be with him. I always felt welcome. And I had no idea that this high school romance would blossom into marriage. In my mind, I would have a wonderful Homecoming date but then be free to date whomever I wanted, especially as we headed to college. But the more time we spent together, the more my heart grew attached to Ben. By the time we graduated from high school and were planning to attend college in separate states, I could not imagine being without him. So we committed to stay together through a long-distance relationship.

My freshman year of college was life-changing for me. God had used Ben's family to plant seeds of the gospel in my heart. By the time I was at college, I knew there was something lacking in my supposed Christian life. I sought out a church and landed at a "come-as-you-are" church plant across the street from my dorm. It was the first time I clearly heard the gospel, and something clicked. There was much I didn't understand, but I knew enough to realize that I was a sinner in need of a Savior. God surrounded me with believers at my 40,000-student secular university. The girls in the dorm room next door began sharing Scripture with me. A young woman from a campus ministry knocked on my door, inviting me out to coffee. She gave me the first Bible I actually read. She discipled me all four years of college.

At the same time, God was working mightily in Ben's life. He originally went to school to become a chemical engineer. But during his freshman year, Ben felt God calling him into full-time ministry. We had numerous heated discussions over the long-distance phone lines, debating what the Bible taught about the roles of men and women. His call to ministry didn't sit well with me. "I don't want to raise our kids in a hut in Africa!" I passionately exclaimed. That was about the extent of missionary life I knew (or thought I knew).

We were at two very different places in our spiritual walks. So just before returning for our sophomore year of college, Ben broke up with me. It was devastating. Why would he break up with me when I was finally a real Christian? I was sad about not only losing Ben, but losing the connection to his family. Barbara and Ron were excited about my newfound faith in Christ. They were eager to hear about my experiences with campus ministry and what I was learning in the Bible.

Ben and I were separated for two years with very little communication. But the irony is that I stayed in contact with Barbara and Ron (I can't recommend this being the right course for every person in the situation I was in, but it is the way my story unfolded, nonetheless). I came home from college on a break and emailed Barbara to see if I could stop by for a visit. I ensured that Ben wasn't there because it was too hard to see him. But I loved how excited his parents were to hear about my relationship with Christ. When I decided to go on an overseas study to Spain, Ron pulled out the world map to see exactly where I'd be. They had become not just the parents of my (ex) boyfriend, but my friends, my brother and sister in Christ.

So, when God led Ben and I back together our senior year of college, I was overjoyed. The Lord had answered my long-awaited prayer. Marrying into a godly, Christian family was a dream come true! Everything should work out smoothly and without conflict because we're all Christians, right?

Despite our committed love to one another the past twenty-plus years, we have faced our share of challenges. From beginning our marriage an ocean away, to figuring out how best to communicate, to the myriad of complexities when children arrived, we've gone through various ups and downs. My idealistic vision at the start of our marriage was replaced with the realities of two sinners who both have their own plans and ideas. And two women who love the same man.

Our First Bump in the Road

Ben and I had broken up for two years. By the time God reunited us, we quickly knew that we wanted to be married. It was agonizing to live hundreds of miles away from each other. We wanted a short engagement so that we could begin our new life together. But there were a few roadblocks in the way. Even though we had both just graduated from college, I still had a year of student teaching remaining. I had received a scholarship to begin working on my master's while student teaching in Michigan. Ben was to begin a pastoral internship in Minnesota. We couldn't fathom being separated one more year, so I began to search out options to student teach in Minnesota. Unfortunately, my college decided they could not set a precedent by allowing me to go out of state. If we wanted to be married soon, I would need to leave my program.

We shared our news with Ben's parents. In a sweet voice Barbara responded, "Don't you think if God provided for Ben to do this internship in Minnesota and provided Stacy with a scholarship in Michigan, that maybe you should wait one more year to be married?" I felt my blood pressure rise as our dream to be married in five months was dashed. Would Ben follow his mom's advice? Would we be forced to go through another agonizing year of a long-distance relationship?

My heart sank as I waited to see how Ben would respond. We considered our various options, but both Ben and I felt strongly that the time to be married was sooner rather than later. Ben told his parents that we were willing to make sacrifices in order to be married that year. We would find another way for me to student teach in Minnesota.

Barbara and Ron were gracious to support our plans. But it was the first realization for my naïve young mind that just because we're all Christians doesn't mean that we'll see everything eye to eye.

Barbara's First Impression

Decades later, I still remember Stacy's bright eyes and sweet smile the first time we talked. Such a beautiful, poised young woman. As she sat across from me in our family room, I wondered, "How could a seventeen-year-old be so comfortable talking with me, a woman more than twice her age?" Stacy was refreshingly different. She asked well-phrased, insightful questions. I expected her to be interested in knowing my son. Was she truly interested in knowing me as well? Clueless, it never occurred to me that she and Ben would one day marry.

Ben is our firstborn. From the moment I knew I was pregnant with him, the course of my life changed. I wanted to be the best mom ever! I read every parenting book I could find. Even better, a mother of five responded to my need for support. This experienced mom became my mentor and friend. My friend's voice of experience helped me grow in confidence to care for my newborn son. This little boy was my life's joy and purpose.

I loved my child more than life itself, but I struggled with doubts. Would there be enough selfless love in my heart for the long haul? Was I even capable of sacrificial love? When I expressed this fear to my friend, she heard my greater need to know God as my Father. She shared the good news that Jesus could heal my broken heart of sin's disease. God is love! He would fill me with his all-powerful life and love and give me all I needed to love my child.

By God's grace, through faith in Jesus Christ, I believed. A new mother, I now was a new child of God. My life's real purpose became clear. My heart filled with faith, hope and love. In God's kindness, within a short time, my husband Ron also trusted Christ. Together, Ron and I began to grow in understanding what it means to follow Jesus.

God had used our firstborn child to lead us to faith in his only Son, Jesus Christ. Then we began to wonder—*What does a Christian family look like?* Though talking to God felt like learning a foreign language, we began to pray for our son. We prayed, not only for his first steps, but for his future. What work would God call him to? Whom would he marry? We asked God, not for a particular job or type of woman, but for our son to do God's will. We prayed his wife would know and love God. Our goal was to equip our son and let him go—not keep him dependent on our care. We wanted to prepare Ben to follow God, not us.

When Ben and Stacy started dating, we had new reasons to pray. How should we respond? Stacy was not a Christian. We didn't have any well-thought-out plan. But we trusted their relationship would end when they left for different colleges. We were wrong! Yet as Ben and Stacy's relationship grew stronger, God was working. Two years later, Stacy again sat in our family room. Joy filled the room as she told us what God had done in her heart and of her newfound faith in Christ.

We were thrilled and relieved—God had resolved our biggest concern. But when Ben and Stacy started talking of marriage, new questions arose. Would they rush ahead too quickly? Would their desire to marry jeopardize Ben's calling to seminary? How would a tender new Christian bear up under the pressure put on a pastor's wife? How would our two families navigate through differences in beliefs and traditions? And to top it off, Ron and I were preparing to move overseas. How would the move impact our relationship with the newlyweds? How would Stacy and I learn to respect and value one another while 10,000 miles apart?

How Our Past Impacts the Present

Another question hit me: What does a good mother-in-law look like? Not like me, I felt sure. Would I fail in this important relationship? I had no example to follow. As a young bride, my mother-in-law never showed interest in me. Perhaps she was simply too tired. Her children's sole provider, she worked extra jobs and sacrificed for others. Even in old age, she cared for her disabled son. I wanted to talk, but I didn't want to hear my mother-in-law's monologue about her struggles. After many years of trying to build a relationship, I gave up. Resentment built in my heart.

My mother and her mother-in-law also had a poor relationship. As a young child, I knew these two important women in my life had no love for one another. Mom enjoyed telling "humorous," hurtful stories about my father's mother—lots of laughs at my grandmother's expense. My mother's strong personality made it hard for my father to love his parents well. Did Dad really have to choose between his parents and his wife? Our family missed the blessing of a woman who embraces her husband's family as her own.

My problem went deeper than a lack of good role models. I was as flawed as my mother and mother-in-law. Before the wedding, someone told me a mother-in-law's job was to "wear beige and shut up." Did this advice apply to the rest of my life? What was I to do? I had reached a turning point. Good examples help, but good examples could not make me a good mother-in-law. Books about relationships may help, but I needed more than a healthy relationship "how-to" manual. I needed my Savior!

Over the past twenty years, new questions still hit my mind and heart, and threaten to disrupt Stacy's and my loving relationship. But I am learning to listen to the questions God has for me. When do I overreact? What have I misunderstood? Why am I more ready to defend than to listen? What sins in my heart would God show me and change through this relationship? I am still a flawed mother-in-law. But in my relationship with Stacy, I have discovered the joy of depending on God—his power and grace—as never before.

Never Without Hope

Our first impressions give us a filter by which we view our future relationship.[1] A positive first meeting can give us hope for a healthy and even close relationship with our future in-law. It might make us eager for the next meeting, when we can continue to get to know one another and build a friendship. Yet a negative first impression can have the opposite effect. A discouraging and disappointing meeting can dash the hopeful thoughts we once had. Instead we might dread the next time we're together—when the next hurtful word might be spoken. But God's Word never leaves us in despair. Even if you have the worst initial impression of your in-law, God's Word gives us hope for change.

Isaiah 43:18–19 tells us, "Do not remember the past events; pay no attention to things of old. Look, I am about to do something new; even now it is coming. Do you not see it? Indeed, I will make a way in the wilderness, rivers in the desert."

Sometimes we can be stuck in a rut of how we view someone, assuming they're always going to be a problem. We replay the hurtful words or inconsiderate actions like a broken record. But this verse from Isaiah 43 challenges us to make a change. Instead of dwelling on all the negative interactions we have had, we are to make an effort to forget them, not even to consider them. We need to believe that God is doing a new thing, starting in our own hearts. He makes a way in the midst of our desert times and gives us reason to hope.

What could this look like in real life? For a daughter-in-law, it could look like picking up when your phone rings with your MIL's number lighting up. It could look like prayerful anticipation when you learn she's coming for a visit. It could look like counting down the days on the calendar with your children to help the whole family anticipate her visit—helping everyone's hearts receive her the way you'd want to be received (or talked about) before entering her home.

On the flip side, what if you're the MIL and it's your DIL who is coming to visit? When the negative memories of unkind words and thoughtless actions come flooding back into your mind, ask God to help you filter your thoughts. Think about what's kind and good and pure (Phil. 4:8). When she comes, notice when she gets things right. And even in the places she doesn't, practice the kind of mercy toward her that you want when you get things wrong sometimes (and the kind of mercy you were given from God—and needed from others—when you were in the green years of marriage or motherhood).

First Corinthians 13:4–7 gives us a great heart check of whether our thoughts toward someone else are loving. Am I being patient and kind? Am I envying or being irritable or insisting on my own way? *Lord, help me to bear all things, believe all things, hope all things and endure all things. Help me make room for her, for this relationship, for the ways you might change us both if we gave some space to trust you with it. Help me trust that you can do something new. Starting with me.* ✎

Discussion Questions

1. What was your first impression of your in-law? How did this experience shape your expectations of the relationship from that point forward?

2. In what situations are you tempted to despair because you are tired of waiting for God to act?

3. What mixture of faith and selfishness do you see in your life?

4. What challenges are you experiencing in your in-law relationship?

5. Have you made a wrong choice in your words or actions that have damaged your in-law relationship?

6. How is God meeting you in your place of sin, loneliness, or hardship?

7. Have you made any room in your head or heart for God to work in your in-law relationship? Or have you closed yourself off, expecting the worst? Why?

BIBLICAL HOPE FOR THE RELATIONSHIP

The Story of Ruth and Naomi

The Most Famous Example

The best-known mother-in-law/daughter-in-law relationship in the Bible is that of Naomi and Ruth. Take a look again at this familiar Old Testament story. Within a few sentences we meet an Israelite family desperate to survive. Famine ravages Bethlehem, their home. Hunger has driven them to Moab, the land of Israel's ancient enemy. After the family's father dies, the sons violate God's law and marry Moabite women, Ruth and Orpah. Then the sons die, leaving Naomi—the mother—and her daughters-in-law with nothing.

For Naomi, Moab now holds only heartache. But in the midst of despair we see God's redeeming grace. Naomi's life has gone all wrong. Yet through all her trials God has kept her faith in him alive. With news of the famine's end in Bethlehem, Naomi decides to return home. Thinking her future holds no hope, Naomi sadly tells Ruth and Orpah her plan.[1] She assumes that going with her isn't in their best interest. Naomi meant well, but she missed what God was doing! God had given her Ruth, a daughter-in-law who loved her. And God would use their relationship to do more than either woman could imagine.

What If the Relationship Looks Hopeless?

Naomi's husband, Elimelech, died, and she was left with her two sons. Her sons took Moabite women as their wives: one was named Orpah and the second was named Ruth. After they had lived in Moab about ten years, both Mahlon and Chilion also died, and the woman was left without her two children and without her husband. . . . "Don't call me Naomi. Call me Mara," she answered, "for the Almighty has made me very bitter. I went away full, but the LORD has brought me back empty. Why do you call me Naomi, since the LORD has opposed me, and the Almighty has afflicted me?" (Ruth 1:3–5, 20–21)

Mara—the Hebrew word for bitter! Naomi so lamented her tragic life that she changed her name to Bitter. "Naomi" means pleasant. But now Naomi's whole identity had changed. How could her life possibly be pleasant ever again? She thought her daughters-in-law should get as far away as possible for their own good. Or, said in her own words, "my life is much too bitter for you to share, because the LORD's hand has turned against me" (Ruth 1:13).

Perhaps you, too, feel the burden of wrong decisions or unexpected suffering. For whatever reason, does it now seem that the LORD's hand has turned against you? Looking back, maybe you see how your choices disrupted your family: different jobs, different cities, new schools, different churches. Or maybe your choices were on the path of wisdom, and you thought you were safe, but then a massive, unwelcome curve ball came and knocked the whole family off course. Goodbye nice, normal, stable family. Hello chaos. Perhaps the dreams for your son (or daughter) to find a nice Christian spouse have evaporated. Maybe the two of them are now married, and you wonder, *Does this new spouse even belong to Jesus?* All you can see is the brokenness. Will this new addition to the family draw your child away from the Lord?

Naomi's life can encourage us. Her family had experienced so much harm. Some of this was due to bad decisions. And some was due to great loss that Naomi couldn't have seen coming—things she didn't cause. In every way, "pleasant" did not describe her life. Things looked hopeless. When we see her depressed nature and prickly personality, we understand why. Could she have prayed more? Should she have tried to persuade her husband to make wiser decisions? Was all this grief self-inflicted? Or was some of this just the reality of life in a fallen world? Whatever part she played in this tragedy, God never abandoned Naomi. Even in the painful loss of her loved ones, God was graciously making himself known. When he called her back to Bethlehem, he was calling her back to himself.

Our failures and imperfections never limit God! In giving Ruth to Naomi, God gave Naomi the opportunity to show Ruth more of his goodness. Perfect decisions, pristine circumstances, and a pleasant personality are not prerequisites for God to use us in our DIL's life either. God doesn't call us to see what he is doing at the level that *he* can see. He simply calls us to trust him. God is writing the story. We get to be part of it. As bad as things looked for Naomi or as bad as they might look for you, the truth is, it's not hopeless. God is involved. Will you trust him? Instead of casting your DIL away, will you see her presence in your life as an opportunity to show the goodness of

God? He will do more than you can imagine. Naomi lacked the right perspective on life and on God. Yet God never stopped pouring out his grace on her life.[2]

A Modern-Day Naomi

Regrets filled Carol's heart. She was going to be the heroine of the story. She was going to bring her DIL, Avery, to faith in Christ. She blamed her own decisions—her own past—for her current crisis with Avery. Her son had missed the advantage and model of a stable home life. Is it any wonder Carol doubted Avery's input? Yet when Carol talked with Avery, she often came away with hurt feelings. "My mother always did it this way." "Oh, I always go to my sister for advice." She wanted so desperately to be a trusted person for her daughter-in-law, but every word out of Avery's mouth seemed like criticism. How often had Carol prayed for God to use her to bring Avery to Christ? Why wouldn't he answer? Now the whole relationship seemed hopeless—and it was all her fault.

When our situation seems hopeless, where can we find hope? If we merely "think positive thoughts" like our culture tells us to do, we are left with false hope. So how can we find true hope? First, we need to recognize that true hope doesn't come from our circumstances changing. We can have hope in God regardless of circumstances. Yet, at the same time, in situations that seem impossible, we learn that God is able! He is able to change things. Yes. He is also able to change *us* in the midst of those things. We can have hope because of our wise and faithful God. Our suffering may seem pointless, but God designed it for our good and his glory. He is using it to pour his strength and love into our lives (Rom. 5:3–5). Whether he changes the circumstances themselves, or simply changes *us* as we face the situation, we can trust that God is up to good things.

Did circumstances change quickly for Carol? No! Some days, she lost hold of the truth of God's goodness and power. Friends advised her, "Just get over it." "Why call her? Just avoid her." Sounds like Naomi's original plan to me. *Just leave her behind. It's better that way.* But God comforted Carol. He invited her to come to him. Some days, Carol could only give God her tears. Yet, day by day, through his Word and his Spirit, God renewed Carol's understanding that he loved her.

Sometimes regret and disappointment still darken Carol's thoughts. But now when she is tempted to bitterness, she prays (Heb. 12:15). God is helping her recognize her wrong reactions. He gives her courage not to try to protect herself by withdrawing from Avery. The Holy Spirit is giving her power. She is learning to hold her tongue. She regularly confesses her wrong thoughts and words to God. Carol may never have that picture-perfect relationship with her daughter-in-law. But the Holy Spirit is freeing her from the need to live up to her image of a perfect mother-in-law. God might not be changing *Avery* in all the ways Carol wants right this moment, but he is clearly changing *her.* Because that's what God does. He transforms.

Today everything may look hopeless in your relationship. What if you feel like your child's marriage is a result of poor decisions you made? What if you realize your personality is more prickly than welcoming? Talk with God. Tell him your heart. Ask him to help you. Your greatest happiness will come when you take him up on what he has freely offered. You will start to see him at work to make your mess something beautiful. *God is always at work doing more than you can imagine!*[3]

I'll love you when I feel like it.

> "Look," said Naomi, "your sister-in-law is going
> back to her people and her gods. Go back with
> her." But Ruth replied, "Don't urge me to leave
> you or to turn back from you. Where you go I
> will go, and where you stay I will stay. Your people
> will be my people and your God my God. Where
> you die I will die, and there I will be buried. May
> the LORD deal with me, be it ever so severely, if
> even death separates you and me." When Naomi
> realized that Ruth was determined to go with
> her, she stopped urging her." (Ruth 1:15–18 NIV)

Full of regrets and love, Naomi tells her daughter-in-law to
stay behind. The life of widows in Moab is hard enough. But
how could her daughters-in-law possibly survive as foreign widows in Israel? No one would want to marry them there. If they
stayed in Moab, they'd have a better shot at remarrying and
starting a new life. Orpah agrees. But Ruth surprises Naomi,
insisting she will go with her.

What can Ruth hope to gain from staying with Naomi?
Ruth is not naive. She knows life will be hard. But she loves her
mother-in-law and she loves her mother-in-law's God. And now
she acts on that love.[4]

What if you have been hurt? Or your in-law is disagreeable?
Maybe she's even unkind. How can you love a woman so unlike
you? She's nothing like the person you dreamed she'd be. Is
there any hope of developing a loving relationship with her?

We enter the mother-in-law, daughter-in-law relationship
expecting what we want—the best. Instead of the dream come
true, suddenly it seems we've ended up in a nightmare. What

can we do? Our unrealistic expectations have only made us super-sensitive. The ugliness of sin smacks us in the face. Our inconsistent feelings mislead us. How can we help but go in the wrong direction? Love has disappeared.

We've been hurt. We pull away. Self-protectively, we watch for more ways she'll miss the mark. We begin to justify ourselves. *She deserves my emotional distance.* Our hearts say, "I'll love my in-law when she stops hurting me." As if love could ever be pain-free! We pretend to love our in-law, but we talk about her behind her back. We find ways to punish her or we take it out on our husbands. Bitterness and cynicism grow. How did we ever think we could stir up love? We give up.

Committed love—what is it? Ruth teaches us the hard truth: committed love is more than a feeling. Feelings are very important and deserve tending to, but true love could never wholly depend on something as unstable as our emotions. For love to be true, it has to be fueled by commitment. Said another way, the true test of love is not if we *feel* it in the moment, but rather if we *show up* to what love requires in the moment. And when we honor the commitment to honor our in-law no matter what, when we show up to what love requires regardless of what the other person is doing, this habit eventually pulls our feelings along toward true love. Whether it's an argument or harsh words, committed love has no room for endless exceptions. True love does not withdraw. Our commitment moves us *toward* the other person in hardship, not away. Love accepts inconsistencies. Ruth loved the real Naomi, not a dream of what she thought she should be.[5]

Modern-Day In-Laws

Sharon has honed her skill at packing criticism into sweet sounding words toward her daughter-in-law, Tara.

"It's so good to hear your voice. I was just wondering when I'd ever hear from you."

"I was so pleased to hear from _____ (the
'good' daughter-in-law) this week. Can you
believe, she always asks for my advice on how
to discipline her kids?"

"Oh goodness, I would have invited you to the
gathering with the others, but I didn't hear
from you at all last week."

To make matters even worse, when Tara tells her husband
about the conversation, all he hears is his mother's sweet voice.
He can't see what is really going on. Would anyone fault Tara
for distancing herself? Is there any hope for love? Neither
Sharon nor Tara feel like loving the other.

Or take the case of Vivian. Problems with her daughter-in-
law, Shelley, surfaced right after the newlyweds returned from
the honeymoon. Vivian tried to think positively about Shelley.
She listed Shelley's strengths. The list stayed short, but her bitterness grew. All she saw were Shelley's annoying rough edges.
More and more, Vivian found herself thinking, *I knew she'd never
change.* Vivian prayed. When things didn't change, Vivian wondered, *Are you listening to me, God?*

We're trapped when we define love as a feeling that we
have no control over. We lock people into categories. Of all
relationships, our culture expects—and even laughs at—
problems between a man's mother and his wife. The worldly
narrative is set for us and we jump right into it.[6] Yet even in
overwhelming difficulties, our feelings don't have to control
us. Having our hormones at the right level may help, but it's
not the key. So, what *is* the key that can unlock the power of
our feelings?

Before the foundation of the world, God in Christ committed to love us. "While we were still sinners, Christ died for us" (Rom. 5:8). Jesus shows us what true love looks like. It follows through on the commitment to love—no matter how costly, and no matter how unworthy the loved one. Committed love does not wait for our in-law to change. It loves first. It loves always. It loves no matter what.

But Jesus's love does even more. His Spirit gives us the power to love. By his grace and for his glory, we can live out our commitment to love. Because he loved us no matter what, we really can love our in-law that way too.

Lord, help, I feel like quitting.

> "The LORD bless him!" Naomi said to her daughter-in-law. "He has not stopped showing his kindness to the living and the dead." She added, "That man is our close relative; he is one of our guardian-redeemers. . . ." When Ruth came to her mother-in-law, Naomi asked, "How did it go, my daughter?" Then she told her everything Boaz had done for her. (Ruth 2:20; 3:16 NIV)

Ruth is hungry. Even if Naomi doesn't seem to be thinking of the next meal, Ruth knows they need to eat. She asks her mother-in-law's permission and leaves to go to a field on the outskirts of the city (Ruth 2:2–3). She joins the others who are poor, in the back-breaking work of gathering the scattered grain the harvesters leave behind.

Where is God in this story? His name is hardly mentioned. Yet, a series of "it just so happened" events unfold. The women happen to arrive as the barley harvest begins. Ruth happens to meet Boaz, who happens to be Naomi's relative. Where is God? We see God everywhere in the book of Ruth. He weaves together every event in the lives of his people for his redemptive purposes in the world.

I (Barb) knew God had called us to missions. Of course, I knew I'd miss my family. I was right; it hurt! I knew culture shock would hit us. I was right; it did. But what I didn't know shocked and hurt me more as we lived out our daily lives in this new area of the world. Why did a simple comment from my coworker make me so angry? Were her words really that harsh? Where did this fear and guilt come from? Day in and day out, the problem wasn't what I was finding out there in the mission field. The problem was what I was finding in *myself*. What was going on with me? With us? Why all this fear, resentment, anger, confusion, frustration, irritation? My husband and I prayed, "God, your guidance seemed so clear. Did we misunderstand you? Do you want us to go home?"

I'd like to say the challenges got easier. That wasn't God's plan! Yet, God assured me he was with us. God opened my eyes to glimpse some of how precisely he was ordering our circumstances. It just so happened event by event, blessings and challenges happened. Ease and struggle came to us, not by chance, but from our Father's loving hand. We had not mistaken God's guidance. We simply failed to understand that God's purpose for us was more than our service. His design always centers on his plan to make us more like his Son. He was doing just as much *in* us as he was through us. God invited me to trust him in a whole new way.

In all truth, God had extended this invitation to me a few months before we even left for the mission field. I'm not talking about the call to be a missionary. I'm talking about becoming a mother-in-law! My son Ben had stood at the altar beaming at

Stacy. I had rejoiced that they were starting a new life together. I knew his relationship with his new bride would take precedence over me, his mother. But boy did I underestimate the cost of living so far away from this new daughter-in-law.

We didn't exchange unkind words. We both tried hard. But I wrestled with the sense that I didn't really know Stacy, and she didn't know me. I felt left out. How could our side of the family be part of this new couple's life together? "Out of sight, out of mind!" Was the old adage really true? Were we out of the loop for good with them? Irrelevant?

"Help, God."

God heard my prayer. Once again, he taught me the basic lesson I've come to learn too many times in my life. I was depending more on my feelings than on God! How many times have I simply prayed, "Make things right"? But God wanted me to ask, "Father, please help me learn to trust you. Make *me* right."

My plans were so small. I thought I understood the big picture. But God's purpose is always greater than we can imagine (Eph. 3:20). Of course, I couldn't see all that God was doing. But I experienced the goodness of his purposes. God was teaching me that he always sees the future with a Father's heart for his child (Ps. 139).

God did not leave me to figure it out. He heard my cry for help and came to me (Gen. 16:13). He lovingly led me by his Word and his Spirit and other good gifts—my husband, pastor, and mentors. I learned anew to lean into God. My love for him grew. I thought God called us to foreign missions to do a work for him. Instead, as I mentioned before, he did a work in us. God did the painful work of showing me more of the pride, anger, and envy in my life. My sin had muddied the beauty of his image in me. I confessed my sins, and his Word brought cleansing (James 5:16; 1 John 1:9).

I knew God's Spirit was transforming my thoughts and desires (Rom. 12:1–2). I honestly prayed, "Father, I am so unlike your beautiful Son. Please make me more like Jesus." I began to pray for Stacy and me, "Father, we are your holy children. Please help us put on compassion, kindness, humility. Lord, please help us be gentle and oh so patient with one another" (Col. 3:12). I knew God was at work, but all too often, the miles magnified the misunderstandings. He had put this distance between us not to hurt us, but for our good. To teach us to lean into him, to trust him, to go to him with something we otherwise wouldn't. I learned to pray, "Lord, you have forgiven me, please help me forgive the same way. And Father help Stacy and me to bear with one another as we grow to love each other. Oh Lord, give each of us a forgiving spirit" (Col. 3:13–14).

God "just so happened" to give me challenges with coworkers the same time he gave my marriage a new work to do in missions. God "just so happened" to give me a new daughter-in-law the same time he moved me across the ocean. None of this was by chance or coincidence. Just like in Ruth's and Naomi's story, God did not make a mistake. He meant to do it. He is on every page of the story. God knew the best way to show his glory and goodness to Stacy and me was to allow the challenges of our relationship to increase. God was weaving our hearts together in love. He was weaving our lives together as part of his plan for the world.

Ultimately, God taught me to celebrate his Providence. When challenges came, I no longer looked for a way out. Though it was painful, I found that more and more my prayers started changing. I started to now ask, "Lord please use me for your purposes in this challenge. Will you make me more like

Jesus? Help me to trust you to use this for my good and your glory. And Lord, please let me show this lost and lonely world the beauty of your Son."

If God can change *me* into a woman who prays that prayer, trust me, he can change *anyone*. He can change you. No matter how the challenges are increasing for you and your in-law, none of it "just so happened." God is the one behind the scenes, lining all the circumstances up just so. He is doing this to help you lean into him. To help you learn how to love like he does. To change you into the image of his Son.[7]

God's Legacy Lives On

> So Boaz took Ruth and she became his wife. When he made love to her, the LORD enabled her to conceive, and she gave birth to a son. The women said to Naomi: "Praise be to the LORD, who this day has not left you without a guardian-redeemer. May he become famous throughout Israel! He will renew your life and sustain you in your old age. For your daughter-in-law, who loves you and who is better to you than seven sons, has given him birth." (Ruth 4:13–15 NIV)

Can you just hear Boaz's family and friends cheer? Boaz steps forward to take the family relative's responsibility to marry the widow Ruth. Naomi begins to hope again for the future of her family. A year later, a baby is born. All the women are in awe of Ruth's love. Together they celebrate the work of God in Naomi's life. Years later, her great-grandson is King David of Israel, whose lineage would lead to the Messiah. Ruth and Naomi's committed love are a living tribute of God's grace. And by God's grace and committed love to us, multitudes of people belong to Ruth's greatest Son, Jesus. What a legacy!

Remember Carol, whose daughter-in-law rejected her? Carol's heart was broken. In frustration, she stayed distant from Avery—yet not distant from God. God was weaving the events of her life together to make her more like his beautiful Son. Avery was not the only one with character flaws! God did a work in Carol. She learned through repentance. God cleansed her from the ugliness of anger, jealousy, and bitterness.

Carol prayed the many highlighted verses in her Bible for Avery often. Although remnants of sadness and regret remained, she prayed: "Be joyful in hope, patient in affliction, faithful in prayer" (Rom. 12:12 NIV). She prayed God would bring Avery to himself.

And God did!

What does all this mean for us? First, it means that whether we are a MIL or DIL, we would do well to remember that the ramifications of decisions made today do not stay bound to today. Even if your in-law has not turned to Jesus for salvation, what you think is the end of the story may not be the end of the story. In a sense, we don't know the true end of the story of Ruth yet because Jesus has not returned yet! Yes, we know he will return. Yes, we know that good will win over evil. But we don't yet know how many people Jesus will be resurrecting to eternal life on that last day, because the story isn't complete yet. People are still coming to know him! If Jesus hasn't returned yet, there is still time for repentance. And so, we must keep in mind that any in-law—whether son or daughter or mother or father—who has turned away from the Lord still has the room to turn back toward him. We must remember and hold to the truth that our God is at work. We can trust him.

Second, it means that we hold to the truth that one of the things God is doing in the story of our in-law relationship is making us more like himself. Even if your relationship with your in-law doesn't mend immediately, God gives his children a precious privilege: to follow in his son's footsteps. Jesus laid down his life for us. He went to the cross for us. Following him never means a pain-free life. We live in a world broken by sin. Some things will not be made right in this life. One thing is sure—God uses even the broken places for the good of his children. He is working in us—changing not just *her;* but *me*—to become different over time, conforming slowly and steadily into the image of his Son, who drew near the very people who raised their fists at him.

Even the challenging, maddening, or complicated experiences with our in-law are opportunities for us to practice Jesus's unfathomable mercy and love for those who seem like they don't deserve it. God always weaves together every event in the lives of his people for their own sanctification and for his redemptive purposes in the world.

Ask God to increase your faithfulness to him. Ask him to build up a love in you that shows up and acts like Jesus no matter what. God will build your trust in him and love for your in-law by giving you faith in even the most trying circumstances. God will meet you and impact generations to come in your family. We do well to consider how God is at work in the very ordinary events and difficult relationships of our life for his greater purposes of redemption. God transformed things for Naomi, Ruth and Boaz—both *in* them and *through* them. God proved himself able in more than they could have imagined—even in the seemingly random or confusing moments that "just so happened." This is what God does![8] ⟵

Discussion Questions

1. What part of Ruth and Naomi's story do you relate to the most?

2. How do you typically define love? Are you living up to that definition? How has this chapter encouraged or challenged your view?

3. When you think of your in-law relationship, where might you be refusing to show up to what love requires, regardless of the other person's actions? Why do you think this is the case?

4. How do these truths from Ruth impact your thoughts and actions toward your in-law who is different from you?

5. Whatever your in-law's situation, God offers you an opportunity to trust him. Will you ask God for faith to trust him?

6. What challenges or blessings in your life feel like they "just so happened"? In what ways is God clearly at work in these situations?

7. In what ways is God doing more *in* you than *through* you right now? What inside of you needs to change?

8. What are you afraid to pray for when it comes to your in-law relationship? What holds you back from consistently running to God in prayer with these desires and requests? How does this chapter speak to this?

LEAVE AND CLEAVE

How Marriage Redefines Relationships

Jen came home from a long day of work, eager to talk with her husband about her day. "Aaron?" she called as she walked in from the garage. The living room was empty and she heard his voice quietly talking from the outdoor patio. As she walked outside to join him, she could tell from the conversation that he was sharing about a stressful situation at the office. "I know, but my boss always ignores every extra effort I make. It doesn't seem worth it. Yeah, maybe you're right. Okay . . . love you too."

Jen could feel her blood pressure rising. He was talking with his mom. Again. She tried to act like it didn't bother her. After all, it's good for men to have healthy relationships with their moms, right? But she was feeling left out. For the entire five years they had been married, Aaron talked to his mom on the phone nearly every day, going emotionally deeper with her than he did his own wife. Jen began to resent the time he spent with her. Why couldn't he come to her for advice about his work situations instead of his mom? It's not that they shouldn't enjoy a close relationship, but why was she still the first person Aaron wanted to talk with? This didn't seem like merely a close relationship. It seemed like a *first place* relationship. Aaron told her she was the most important person in his life. But it sure didn't feel like it.

Aaron's overly-enmeshed relationship with his mom was hindering him from being one with his wife. Jen started to feel like she was in competition with his mom, who always seemed to be clamoring for Aaron's attention through phone calls, texts, or drop-in visits. Issues that Jen wished Aaron would discuss with her, he had already talked through with his mom. He was so ready and willing to take her advice. Jen began to wonder if the man she married was capable of breaking off an unhealthy dependence on his mom. And she wondered if he truly loved her as much as he said he did?

The First Relationship

In the book of Genesis God introduces us to the first human relationship ever mentioned: marriage. After God creates the heavens and earth, the land, sea, and animals, God creates man in his own image (Gen. 1:26). He decides that it's not good for man to be alone, so he creates a helper fit for him (Gen. 2:18). Out of Adam's own rib, God creates a woman to be by his side. It is this story, all the way back in the beginning, that gives precedent for how all marriages should function: "This is why a man leaves his father and mother and bonds [or 'cleaves'] with his wife, and they become one flesh" (Gen. 2:24). It's interesting to note that woman was created from man, from the same body, from *one flesh*. And so in a sense, when a man and woman get married, they're moving from being separate to returning to their original state at creation.

The principle derived from this verse is often called "leave and cleave." It's a commonly used phrase in Christian circles when discussing marriage. But what exactly does it mean? Does leaving mean cutting off ties with your parents?

In Hebrew, the word *leave* in Genesis 2:24 means to forsake dependence on, depart from, let go, or release. The word *cleave* or *hold fast* means to join, cling to, stick to, or stay close.[1] Think of how glue can hold two pieces of paper together to look like one piece. That's what cleaving is intended to do. Two separate people becoming one in their covenant commitment in Christ. Jesus reiterates the command in Matthew 19:5–6, "and he also said, 'For this reason a man will leave his father and mother and be joined to his wife, and the two will become one flesh.' So they are no longer two, but one flesh. Therefore, what God has joined together, let no one separate." No one is supposed to come between husband and wife.

In Ephesians 5:29–31, Paul reiterates this command with the parallel of Christ and the church. Husbands are to love their wives as their own bodies. "For no one ever hates his own flesh but provides and cares for it, just as Christ does for the church, *since we are members of his body*. For this reason a man will leave his father and mother and be joined to his wife, and the two will become one flesh" (italics added). Paul is quoting Genesis 2:24 to show that Christ and the church are one body. The union of man and wife in marriage points to the reality of the union between Christ, the last Adam, and his bride, the church.[2] (The point is further illustrated in 1 Corinthians 6:16 when Paul says whoever unites himself with a prostitute becomes "one body" with her.)

A marriage reveals two distinct people that are simultaneously considered one unit. They are diverse as separate people, but they are united as one flesh. This is similar to the unity and diversity we see in the church body. As 1 Corinthians 12 shows us, each member of the body of Christ has its own unique quality, showing us that the church is comprised of diverse parts. Yet, at the same time, they are *one* unified body—no one part can be separated from the whole. They each have different characteristics yet are melded together as one. This is why Paul can say that the people in the church are corporately considered "the body of Christ" as a whole and at the same time, we are "individual members of it" (1 Cor. 12:27). We don't have to choose between being united or being diverse; we're both. In much the same way, a husband and wife are two separate people with different gifts, ideas, personalities and passions, yet in the marriage union, they become one flesh. Not only do they become one flesh through sexual union, but they meld their ideas and beliefs as they form a new family entity.[3]

Marriage as a New Identity

Sue said, "The best thing that my mother-in-law ever did for me was when we got married, she LET HIM GO! She told us that she will not be meddlesome, or overbearing, and that she did the best she could raising him, and understood it was time to let him live his life with his new wife and family."

Leaving your parents and becoming one with your spouse requires a new identification as a married couple. A new family has been formed and a separation must take place. There's a shift in responsibility as the parents step back from being the first line of defense with physical, financial, and emotional provision, and the new couple steps forward into its rightful place of being a first line of defense for their new family unit.

When Stacy came on the scene as my first daughter-in-law, as with any "first," I had a lot to learn. A good mother-in-law is not ready-made but a work in progress! Much of what I know today is the result of trial and error (many errors). I've also learned a lot from friends who want to be good and godly mothers-in-law. This is the highest truth I've learned: the marriage relationship comes first. This means a new couple needs time alone to get to know how to relate to one another. They don't need a lot of third-party influence!

A strong marital bond eventually leads to a flourishing family. What more could a mother-in-law want? Yet many marriages do not bond because the new couple does not "leave" the emotional ties to parents and in-laws. The new bond needs time to set—"cleave." A married couple thrives best as they learn to rely on each other. This doesn't mean that married couples must disappear, neglect, or totally cut off the relationship with their parents, driving away to never be seen again. It means that parents and in-laws learn to take the back seat—not only in the car but in decision-making conversations! We've had years to instruct, model, and coach. Now it's time to loosen our grip and let the new relationship take hold. And that relationship, too, along with its decisions, will have many trials and errors. And that's okay—in fact, that's exactly what a new married couple needs to learn the ropes of how to do life together as one unit.

As pastor-theologian John Piper says, we can draw out four aspects of a new marriage that separates it from former participation in the larger familial household. The first aspect is one of *allegiance*. When a man and woman marry, there is now a new "allegiance, devotion, affection, intimacy, and priority" on the part of the husband and wife. This new marriage takes first place in their lives (apart from their devotion to the Lord, of course). The second through fourth aspects fall under the umbrella of *responsibility*. There's a new structure of responsibility for who bears the primary burden of *providing materially* for the family, *protecting* the new family, and *providing leadership* in this new unit of marriage—namely, the husband. "Those new structures of allegiance and responsibility necessarily lead to a kind of leaving mother and father—leaving old structures of allegiance, old structures of provision, old structures of protection, old structures of leadership," Piper says. "At least that much is built into the very nature of what the New Testament describes as marriage."[4]

In Ephesians 5 Paul parallels the husband being the head of the wife to Christ being the head of the church. Just as Christ nourishes and cherishes the church, giving himself up for her, so husbands are to sacrificially love their wives. This change in family headship would obviously impact how the new married couple will relate to their parents.

Dave Harvey puts it this way, "Once a couple gets married, there's a seismic shift in the parents' role. They don't stop being Mom and Dad, but they can't expect to be honored the same way they were when the kids were young. How time is spent, the frequency of being together, where holidays happen, expectations for seeing grandchildren, the way counsel or opinions are shared—all of these glorious blessings must move out of the realm of expectation and into the realm of collaboration."[5]

Emma shared with me a story of she and her husband's first Christmas together as a married couple. "We decided to try to please both sides of the family by traveling cross-country to spend Christmas with my in-laws, and then traveling cross-country in the other direction to be with my parents. My mother-in-law insisted that all nine of their children stay with them, along with the spouses of those who were married. We were stuffed in the house with no privacy. On Christmas morning, my mother-in-law wanted to continue her family tradition of having all of her children line up according to their birth order to receive their stocking. When I went to get in line with my husband, I was told I couldn't stand with him! It was just for the original family. I know it sounds silly, but it felt hurtful. Instead of my mother-in-law seeming happy to welcome me into the family, I felt like an outsider. Add the stress of too many people in one house and the chaos of holiday traveling, my husband and I vowed to never travel again at Christmas. We would stay home and do our own thing."

Before marriage, parents likely expected their children to be together for holidays, vacations, and other important events. But after marriage, there is a new family to consider. Does the spouse want to be with her parents for Christmas? Does the new couple want to create their own family traditions, and not be bound by the expectations of parents and in-laws? As Harvey points out, these blessings move out of the realm of expectation and into the realm of collaboration. The first priority is no longer what the parents want, but what is best for the new family. Maybe they will split time between both sides of the family for holidays. Or maybe they will decide it is too stressful to travel and try to please everyone at Christmas, and they'll opt to have a quiet Christmas at home with their immediate family. Either way, expectations change to collaboration as both sides work together to develop a new plan.

If you're a mother-in-law or father-in-law, none of this means that your opinions don't matter. None of this means that you can't express your desires. It simply means that your traditions and desires are no longer the deciding vote on how your child's new family goes about things. You've had your window of time to build those traditions the way you deemed best, and you were blessed with the ability to make some memories. But now it is time for a new family to have *their* window of time to build some things they want to build in the ways *they* deem best. It's time for them to make their own memories—to be given the chance to have a say in how their family unit moves through life and special occasions. The traditions you hold dear are dear to you because you had the chance to create them in the first place. Give them that chance. Give them the ability to create some things dear to them, too—things they get to put their handprints on and call their own.

Pursuing Oneness

A primary goal of biblical marriage is to pursue oneness as a couple, in order to be a picture of Christ and the church (Eph. 5:21–33). To do so, we need to reevaluate what it means to leave and cleave. When we leave our family of origin and enter into a new marriage, we're readjusting our focus so that nothing hinders our primary covenant commitment with our spouse. Does my spouse know without a shadow of a doubt that they're the most important person in my life? Does my relationship with my parents have too much influence in my life? Does my spouse feel threatened by how close I am to my parents? Failure to "leave" our parents deprives any couple of the intimacy intended for marriage.

As we learn to cleave, we need to evaluate every new opportunity that comes our way. We need to ask ourselves, will this activity hinder my desire to cherish and love my spouse? Leaving and cleaving isn't a one-time event, but something couples constantly need to be aware of in their marriage. When major life transitions happen like a move or child being born, it can be easy to fall back into the typical patterns of dependence with parent and child. There's a temptation for the young couple to become overly dependent on Mom and Dad, whether that be emotional or financial. And there's a temptation for the parents to hang on too tightly to the relationship, giving advice that's never been sought. This isn't just a principle for newlyweds, but one that needs to be maintained throughout married life.

Marriage changes the way adult children relate to their parents. Leaving takes place in a variety of ways, including emotional and financial dependence.[6]

Emotional Dependence

Children grow up depending on their parents to provide for their needs, both physical and emotional. We look to our parents to give us comfort when we're sad, advice on what career to pursue, and to provide the resources we need to live. This is not an easy change for many MILs. As a mom says good-bye to that relationship with her son, there can be a wrestling match in her heart. She knows he is grown and needs to move on without her help! But what if they make mistakes? What if they make plans that don't include her? What if they decide on something she wouldn't choose? I (Barb) had to learn to let go of the parental role so our son and his new bride could live out their own callings from God. I had to learn that when a couple marries, much of what my support used to look like needed to change.

Think back to our example of Aaron and Jen. Aaron obviously has a close relationship with his mom and relies on her counsel and support. But that very relationship is threatening his relationship with his wife. Aaron's everyday conversations with his mom make his wife feel like she is second best, and being left out of important discussions. If something doesn't change, a root of bitterness will spring up between Jen and Aaron's mom. Family gatherings or special holidays won't be something to look forward to because it will feel like a competition for Aaron's attention.

My husband and I (Stacy) have been thankful to be able to go to our parents with some heavy concerns. It means the world to know that our parents are interceding on our behalf and will faithfully hold us up in prayer. When a ministry situation is rough or a child is in trouble, we've counted on the support and prayers of our parents. But we've always discussed the issues at length as a couple before going to our parents for counsel and prayer. Our parents are a secondary line of defense, not the first line of defense. They stand with us in the gap, not for us.

In another example, let's look at a different couple with a different situation—Sandra and Jake. Sandra and Jake have experienced a lot of marital tension. From different ideas of where to live, to how to spend their money to arguments over what to do on the weekend, their marriage has been wrought with difficulty. Sandra is thankful to have a close relationship with her mom. When Jake has been difficult, or made spending decisions that aren't made the way Sandra would have made them, Sandra can count on her mom to listen to her heartache and give her advice.

Sandra's mom has an increasing dislike for Jake. She can't believe how immature he is, from the way he spends money so carelessly to never taking Sandra's feelings into consideration. She can't help but feel bitterness and resentment rising up between her and her son-in-law. And now he wants to take a job in a different state, moving Sandra, and any future grand-children, hundreds of miles away from her. She can't believe the selfishness in his heart. Doesn't he realize how important it is to live near family? Doesn't he know it would break Sandra's heart to move so far away?

Do you see what's happening here? The closeness between Sandra and her mom has created division in the marriage. Sandra depends on her mom for comfort, help, and a listening ear. But her mom's willingness to listen to negative things about Jake creates bitterness between herself and her son-in-law. Even when Sandra claims Jake has changed and things are better, her mom is still suspicious. Is Jake really making wise choices with their money? Has he really considered Sandra's feelings about the move?

Jake felt like Sandra's mom had too much control in their relationship. She would use her close relationship with Sandra to manipulate situations. He wondered whether he could really take the new job in another state without being laden with guilt. Sandra's emotional dependence on her mom put a wedge in the marriage relationship.

Advocate for the Marriage, Not Only Your Child

The relationship between parent and child is unique, especially with a mother. Mothers have carried the baby in their womb for nine months, perhaps fed their baby with their own body, sacrificed sleep for the sake of the baby's needs, and watched their child grow and change. They've kissed the boo-boos and driven to hundreds of games and practices. They've counseled their first broken hearts and celebrated every victory. The bond between mother and child will be different than the bond between in-law and child.

Because of the natural love for your child, if you're a mother-in-law, it can be easy to fall into the pattern of giving preferential treatment to your son or daughter. You're naturally going to side with their plight, just like Sandra's mom did. That's why it can be so dangerous to even listen to negative talk about their spouse. Suddenly the parent is put in the position of judge instead of friend. It's tempting to choose sides, or try to manipulate the situation in your favor. And the bitterness that can spring up toward your child's spouse is dangerous.

Parents need to make a conscious effort to advocate for their child's marriage, not only their child. They need to look for ways to help their child stay united with their spouse instead of siding with only their child's point of view. If the adult child is in a pattern of verbally tearing down their spouse, it's time to stop the gossip.

Sometimes stopping the gossip looks like encouraging the child to go to marriage counseling, or finding other trusted mentors in the church, but regardless, parents must remember their goal should be the same as their children's goal—to help them pursue oneness in marriage. Other times, stopping the gossip doesn't look like pointing your child to outside help like counseling or mentors (though that's certainly a good idea) but handling critical words about a spouse by offering motherly, biblical counsel right there in the moment. And the key word is *biblical*. Any of us can offer a listening ear and welcoming arms to those we love, but what makes counsel truly wise and restorative in moments like these is if it comes from Scripture, which is an agent of life, change, and help in times of trouble. The goal isn't tearing down, but building up. The question is this: How can you offer biblical advice that moves this couple toward restoration and unity instead of division? (In rare situations, parents might be being alerted to a dangerous or abusive situation. In this scenario, the parents have a unique privilege of counseling their child toward physical safety if needed.)

How does a mom learn to let go? One day, like a light switch turning on in my heart—I (Barb) thought, *What if I take my concerns for this newly married couple to God?* I know that prayer is God's invitation for me to join him in the work he is doing. I had enjoyed praying for Ben and Stacy as individuals. It was time to pray for the couple—joy in one another; appreciation of each other's strengths, and patience with differences. I asked

God to help them enter into the newness of an expanded family. Warming up to new in-laws, brothers-in-law, and sisters-in-law is not always easy. Yet prayer is one way to warm your heart up to a new relationship. It's hard to stay distant or cold toward a person you are praying for daily!

Financial Dependence

Leslie and Jim were on a tight budget. With three small children, college loans, and entering into full-time ministry, they knew they'd be strapped when it came to money. Leslie's parents were well off and were happy to bless their daughter's young family with things they couldn't afford—taking them out to dinner, new clothes for the kids, even generously paying for their vacations. Leslie and Jim were thankful for the help. But it seemed like with each new gift, the expectations were growing.

Leslie shared with me about their dilemma: "My parents are offering to give us their SUV. It would be such a blessing. We really need the space and our cars are constantly needing repairs." With a pause and a concerned look on her face, she then went on: "I'm just worried that it will come with an expectation to go see them each time a holiday rolls around. My mom even reminded me that with the SUV, we would have a reliable car to drive there this Christmas. Jim feels uneasy about accepting the gift. He notices that the strings attached keep getting longer and longer."

Can you see what the problem is? Leslie's parents were very generous, but it came with strings attached. Jim and Leslie knew if they accepted the vehicle there would be pressure to go to her parents for the holidays. Were her parents encouraging oneness and unity in their marriage by providing financial relief? Or were they serving their own interests by manipulating the situation?

Or consider my friend Anna, and her husband, Jamal. They have a growing young family. His parents both worked blue-collar jobs and struggled to make ends meet. They realized Jamal's potential at a young age and did everything they could to afford him the best education possible. When it was time for Jamal to go to college, he was accepted at a prestigious, and expensive, university. Jamal's parents didn't have the means to help with tuition, but he decided to attend even with the uncertainty of his finances. Jamal completed two years of college before running out of money and dropping out. But his bright mind gave him an idea for a new business. Jamal and Anna sacrificed much as they got the business off the ground, and now Jamal is a successful entrepreneur.

Over the years Jamal has sent large sums of money to his parents. Sometimes they had an unexpected medical bill, or his dad was out of work, or they needed rent money. Anna has tried to be understanding but feels bitterness growing in her heart each time she sees Jamal writing a check to them. "I don't know how to get Jamal to stop sending money to his parents. I'm glad we can help them, but it seems over the top. When can we start saving for our own family?"

Do you see what's happening in this situation? The new couple, now barely starting out on their own, is now responsible for not only their own financial health, but their parents' financial health as well. While Jamal's new job is a wonderful thing and his generosity should be applauded, the provision his job offers may not be able to spread across the amount of people who are banking on it to get them through.

The truth of the matter is that the financial norms and expectations within any given family unit change from family to family due to a variety of factors—geographical location, socioeconomic status, cultural differences, and so on. But regardless of how those norms play out in any given marriage, one aspect of leaving and cleaving is through financial independence. On one hand, if the young married couple is still depending on Mom and Dad to bail them out of financial hardships, it leaves an unhealthy dependence on the parents. The couple might get used to overspending, knowing Mom and Dad are there to provide relief. It could prevent the husband from fully taking the responsibility to provide for his family. And with a continuing financial investment in the new family, the parents will likely feel some right to know how their money is being spent, or want to weigh in on financial decisions. This does not mean that in-laws can never give a generous gift over the course of a lifetime, but it does mean that every financial exchange between the two parties should be treated with thoughtful and rigorous consideration.

On the flip side, if the older parents are putting too much pressure on the younger couple to help them along, the younger couple likely can't float that many people at once. This is especially true when a couple is in their early years, feeding many little mouths (or lots of student debt) on an entry-level salary. While generosity is certainly a biblical principle and should be obeyed (and celebrated), a couple pressed too far may end up putting themselves in an unsustainable situation in two directions—both their parents won't be able to get along in life, nor will their own new family unit. In this situation, the same principle holds true: every financial exchange between two parties should be considered carefully and compassionately from both sides.

No matter your upbringing or culture, finances can easily be a source of contention. Whether it's different approaches to budgeting, what car to buy, or whether to accept a generous financial gift from a parent or a child, money is often a source of conflict in marriage. These decisions are difficult to make between a husband and wife with a strong marriage, but add in the dynamic of in-laws, and things get even messier.

Living on Love and Wedding Money

My husband and I (Stacy) married young. We had just finished college, and Ben was preparing for ministry. He had an internship at a church while working part-time as a meter-reader (the faster he ran, the more money he made!). I was student teaching for a semester before looking for my first real job. We had negative income! We liked to say that we were living on love and wedding money. But even in our blissful poverty, we knew that we were on our own. And it was a bonding, unifying experience. Mom and Dad would not be paying our rent, or our car insurance, or our grocery bill. This was part of becoming a new family.

One sunny spring day I was driving our Dodge Dynasty to my student teaching location. As I neared the exit ramp, the car started sputtering and chugging. I pulled off to the side of the ramp, wondering what to do. This was the age before cell phones existed. After an inspection by the local mechanic, we realized that we had burned out the engine. Let's just say that both of us were pretty clueless on how to take care of a car. It was a frightening experience. We didn't have the funds to purchase a replacement. What were we going to do? We asked the Lord to provide, and he heard our prayer. Another couple in the church loaned us their second car while we got our engine rebuilt. Not having Mom and Dad there to bail us out actually increased our faith and dependence on the Lord. *He* was our provider, not our parents.

As we mentioned before, it's alright to accept a gift every now and then, but ultimately, adult children need to be ready and willing to work hard and provide for their own family. There shouldn't be an expectation that the parents will keep supporting them once they have flown the nest. (Nor should there be an expectation the other way around—that flying the nest automatically obligates the adult children to cover any and all expenses in their extended family.) It's not that one side or the other can't occasionally give a generous gift, but can they do it without strings attached?

If you're in the position of being generous with your in-law, you need to ask yourself, "Can I freely give this gift without expectations attached?" If the answer is no, it's better not to give the gift than risk becoming bitter or angry. Another good question to ask is, "Is the current level of our financial help to the other party making us negligent providers for the needs within our own walls?" If so, there may be a level of unhealthy codependence.

On the flip side, if you're in the receiving position, you too must ask yourself, "Can we receive this gift without feeling either indebted or entitled—which might lead to compromise or division in our family?" Or, "will accepting this gift fuel a bad habit we've created of *not* planning for this particular need in our lives? Does this gift help us continue in our negligence in this area of our budget? If accepting the gift will tether you to the other party in a controlling way, or if it furthers negligence in your budgeting, it's better to politely decline the offer.

Leave, Cleave, and Honor Your Parents

The Bible clearly instructs us to separate from Mom and Dad while uniting with our spouse. Yet, at the same time, it also tells us to honor our parents (Exod. 20:12). So, if you're the daughter-in-law in your family, how do you "leave and cleave" while still honoring your parents? The good news for us is that the two are not at odds! We really can do both. Here are a few simple ways that we can still honor our parents while keeping our marriage relationship primary:

1. Words

The tongue is powerful. The book of James compares it to the bit that guides the horse and the rudder that steers the ship (James 3:3–4). And it warns us that an entire forest is set ablaze by the power of the tongue (James 3:6). How do our words reflect our relationship with our in-laws? It can be easy to join the crowd in voicing our complaints and misgivings. When I (Stacy) was doing research for this book, I had a dinner date with a small group of women. When I asked if any of them would be willing to talk with me about their relationship with their mother-in-law, it was met with a chorus of laughter and groans. It's typical to complain about the unkindness or intrusiveness of your in-law. But what if we changed the expectation?

What if instead of voicing how she disappointed us, we shared something we appreciated about her? One way to honor our in-laws is to speak well of them, whether they deserve it or not. Even in the hardest of relationships, we can find something to be grateful for. She birthed and raised the man you chose to marry, right? For example, even if you don't like the kinds of gifts that you or your children receive, you can appreciate your MIL's generosity and thoughtfulness. On the flip side, if you're the MIL, your DIL is the one your beloved son chose to marry. If he finds her special, can you also look for the lovely things about her? Use your words to affirm the good things you see your in-law doing, instead of voicing your complaints. Find ways to affirm your in-law personally and publicly, whether speaking well of her at a lunch date together, in front of a group of friends, or praising her on social media. There are multiple ways to let your in-law and others know you love them and value their relationship. We all know Ephesians 4:29 calls us away from the kind of talk that tears down, telling us instead to speak in ways that are "good for building up, as fits the occasion, that it may give grace to those who hear" (ESV).

What if you intentionally tried this with your in-law? I think we'd all be surprised at how much this could change the tone of the relationship over time.

2. Time

How we spend our time reveals what's important to us. If you live close to your in-laws, do you make it a point to see them regularly? Lives are busy and full, especially with children. But could you drop by with the kids when you're out running errands? Or maybe have a regular meal together each month? There are lots of ways that can demonstrate your love and care by the time you spend with them. Many of us don't live close to our in-laws. But we have wonderful gifts of technology to be able to connect. Can you text your mother-in-law to let her know you're thinking of her? Can your kids FaceTime with their grandparents to catch them up on their lives? What about the old-fashioned phone call or having your kids write a note to send in the mail? These little efforts go a long way toward a healthier relationship. Yes, it feels inconvenient. Yes, it will cost you time and energy. But what relationship doesn't?

To put yourself in your MIL's shoes, just think of your own kids. Think of all the energy you have poured into their every season of life. Think of all the unseen moments you sacrifice for them and help them along in life. Think of all that time invested. Wouldn't you want your kids, years down the line, to pause and give you some intentional time in return? Wouldn't you want to be valued? Remembered? Honored? After all those years of planting seeds in your child's heart, wouldn't you want to delight in the fruit of your labor, enjoying the person they've blossomed into when they're all grown up? Of course you would. Of many things, that's what sacrificing your time is—letting your MIL enjoy the fruit of her labor.

If you're a MIL, perhaps offer to babysit or initiate toward a lunch date with just you and your DIL. Send a card just because. Text her every now and then to ask how work is going. Write her a letter, or send her an article on a subject she's interested in. Depending on how far apart you live, ask if a quarterly or biannual visit could work, where you go to them instead of asking them to take off work and pack up a van full of child gear and incessant screaming to come to you. Put yourself in her shoes. Think back to how hard life could feel in those middle years when you were pulled in a million directions. Just old enough to take care of little kids, just young enough to take care of older parents, and just established enough to receive endless requests to volunteer at church, school, and little league. In the building stages of career and family, where long hours are required. Up all night with tummy bugs and then up all day with the next day's demands, managing so much that you always feel like you're disappointing someone. What did you need in that exhausting season of life? Most likely, encouragement. So when you give your time to your DIL, even if it's in short spurts, remember that's what you're doing—you're giving encouragement and support in a season she desperately needs it!

However it looks, making communication and time with your in-laws a priority reveals your love and care for them. It shows you are willing to put yourself in their shoes, and give them what you'd want in that situation.

3. Tangible Help

In some cases, younger in-laws or grandparents still have the energy or strength to help their adult children with various things like house projects or babysitting. We've (Stacy) been the happy recipients of my father-in-law's handiness around the house or help with the kids when we needed an anniversary trip sans kids. Whether it's a meal provided after having a baby, help with moving or putting together an event, or expertise in a certain hobby, MILs have the opportunity to be such a treasure in all sorts of ways, given how much wisdom they have accumulated over the years. The trick is being willing to ask for it! Many DILs struggle with asking for tangible help because they feel the pressure to be super mom. They think they are supposed to be able to do it all. Might I encourage you, if you're a daughter-in-law, to take a chance and ask for help in the places you need it?

On the flip side, as our parents age, we'll need to get more comfortable with not just receiving help, but giving it. For example, health problems will inevitably come to our parents. There's often a reversal of roles as adult children need to help aging parents. This year I (Stacy) flew home for a week to help my mom recover from open-heart surgery. I cooked as many meals as I could and stocked their freezer with easy-to-warm-up dinners. It was a strange role reversal, but one that I was more than happy to do. At some point adult children will realize they need to be the ones offering physical help with the yard, or house projects or running errands for their elderly parents. This is a good and right way to honor the parents who have sacrificed so much as they raised us (1 Tim. 5:4, 8).

4. Prayer

What better gift can we give to our in-laws than to pray for them? Through our regular communication with them, we know their needs and desires. And we can boldly bring them before the throne of grace, interceding on their behalf. I (Stacy) love knowing that I have a praying mother-in-law. When the pressures of life and ministry surround us, it's a gift to know I can share my burdens with Barb. She is a faithful prayer warrior. Sharing prayer requests is a way our relationship is deepened as we entrust our hearts to one another. Even if your in-law is not a believer, the most loving thing you can do is pray for them to come to know the true and living God. And, there's always the perk that praying for an in-law naturally softens your heart toward them. If you want a better heart toward your MIL or DIL, praying might help you even more than it helps them! ✐

> Don't worry about anything, but in everything, through prayer and petition with thanksgiving, present your requests to God. (Phil. 4:6)

Discussion Questions

1. What does it mean to "leave and cleave"?

2. How does marriage create a new identity?

3. How have you pursued oneness in your marriage? How can you help your adult children pursue oneness in their marriage?

4. What are some practical ways that MILs can advocate for their DIL's marriage?

5. What are the dangers of a couple being emotionally or financially dependent on their parents (or vice versa)? What are the dangers of this for the parents? Are there any unhealthy emotional or financial ties in your in-law relationship? What's a good next step for addressing those?

6. How can you (DIL) honor your in-laws and parents while still leaving and cleaving to your spouse? How can you (MIL) be generous and loving toward your child's marriage while still allowing them to leave and cleave together?

7. This chapter listed four ideas for honoring your in-laws: words, time, tangible help, and prayer. In which of these four are you strongest? Weakest? How might you take a small step toward developing the area you feel weakest in?

EXPECTATIONS

Everyone Has a Dream

As retirement approached, I (Barb) dreamed of the perfect celebration to mark the occasion—a family gathering. In younger years, I considered getaways to be just that—*getting away* from job, kids, and responsibilities. Ron and I enjoyed the pursuit of many adventuresome dreams. Exotic destinations sometimes heightened the anticipation. But most times we preferred to celebrate—just the two of us—with a weekend away anywhere out of our zip code. Now, all these years later, life's bucket list is short and family gatherings are at the top. We don't want to get *away* from all our relationships, we want to get *together*. We realize how precious those moments are, and we want to create lasting memories.

A friend of mine shared about his parents' commitment to a yearly family get-together. This gathering was now a favorite tradition. He joyfully anticipated catching up with his brothers and sisters-in-law. The cousins—now best of friends—counted the days until their next time together. This left me wondering if other families did something similar, so I asked around. My informal survey proved that most friends with grown children planned regular opportunities for their family to meet. Asked why they pour out the effort and expense, the hands-down response: "Years fly by and families grow apart. The investment reaps precious dividends of stronger family relationships."

I started to dream in color—celebrating with those I love most. Christmas school holidays seemed like the right time. But December requires extra ministry responsibilities for all my kids' families. (If you've ever worked in the church world, you know that Christmas for ministry folks tends to deplete everyone's energy reserves.) Navigating crowded airports with multiple children is anything but relaxing. Few joyfully anticipate sleeping on a different pillow and eating who knows what. And what about those flu bugs raging through families like an out-of-control forest fire? Yet, I had my dream of celebrating retirement *and* starting a new family tradition, and I was going to see it through.

✧

A couple years ago, Barb's dream materialized. She and Ron generously flew my (Stacy) entire family to California for this Christmas/retirement celebration. We were all staying in the same house together—our family of six, my sister-in-law's family of five (with three young children) along with Barb and Ron. We were excited to be together in a beautiful location for a week, all thirteen of us. The kids were eager to see their cousins, special plans being made for what to do each day, even foods and diets discussed. But it didn't take long before there was trouble in paradise.

Upon arrival, we learned that my sister-in-law's children had been fighting the stomach flu. Obviously, bathrooms were being shared, and my internal alarm bells went off. Memories of the last Christmas we had all been together flashed in my mind—the stomach flu knocking out family members one by one. How would I protect my family from getting sick? Especially my five-year-old who was so excited to play with his cousins? Differences in diet and a no-sugar policy for one family had us all wondering how this would work. Could you really have Christmas without cookies?

My MIL and SIL had been thoughtful to buy us desserts to have once the sugar-free children went to bed. We must have done a bad job hiding the sweet, because the kids quickly got a whiff of the chocolate and ice cream, and when bedtime arrived, meltdowns started happening.

Sharing beds and rooms (for the kids) meant that no one was sleeping well. And different internal alarm clocks were waking people up at various hours of the night. None of this left any of the adults at our best during the daytime hours. As we tried to decide on what excursions to go on, and entered the chaos of getting thirteen people ready to leave at the same time, frustrations rose. Did we all need to be together *all* of the time? How do you pace a family bike ride when the kids ride at various speeds and have different levels of ability? Did we have the freedom to leave on an excursion without the entire group?

The Fall of Barb's Reality

After my dream took shape, planning began. Many times, I plan to a fault. Like a playwright who turns an idea into a complete story, I began to write mental notes of various scenes. I started giving people lines, and even though no one had access to this script I was preparing in my own mind, I expected everyone to memorize those lines.

The day arrived. The house was full. But my best plans could not anticipate all the needs in this group of thirteen. Unique individuals. Differing parenting styles. Various dietary demands. Thirteen sleeping schedules. It didn't take long to realize that each person in this precious family came with their own dreams.

We had all gladly exchanged cold climates for bright sunshine and warm breezes. One sunny afternoon, we rented bicycles and biked down the seaside trail. What fun to see smiles and hear giggles. I was in a glorious mood. About half-way along the trail, I realized the mood of one family was not nearly as sweet as my own. Our son and daughter-in-law's family was not happy. As they turned to go in another direction, I thought, *How could they think only of themselves and not the fun of us all? Why can't we all stay together?*

I had anticipated we would all share the same happy mood. Sure, other families struggle to enjoy each other. But us? Surely not. I assumed, "Our family is different. No problems. Good relationships." My eager-to-encourage-and-support attitude said, "If I plan enough, and try really hard, all will be well." Problem was, they hadn't read their script. I was surprised and hurt.

The Death of Stacy's Dream

Before we left for that vacation, I (Stacy) had it in my head that it was going to be a California Christmas adventure. Like Barb, I had my own dreams and scenes in mind when I pictured our time away. I had an expectation that everyone would be healthy, that there would be some flexible time for each family each day, and that overall, that we would have a fun and relaxing time together. The chaos of our daily life with four kids and full-time ministry leaves us longing for a much-needed rest. And sunny California seemed like the perfect place.

When our five-year-old started throwing up, we were already lacking good sleep. Now we were even more deprived. Temper tantrums seemed to be the norm. Everyone felt pressure to be together all the time instead of enjoying flexible time. All my ideal plans were lost. My dream shattered. My feelings of anger and resentment seemed justified. Could this really be called a vacation?

Looking back, I can see now that I had allowed my good desires to become ultimate, and that I too, expected everyone else to follow the script in my own head. My worship had turned to whining. And lots of unsavory words and emotions were tumbling out.

Good Desires Turned Bad

Among many situations, the holidays create the perfect storm for unmet expectations. It is common practice for families to gather together for special dinners, gift exchanges, and various traditions. Long hours of traveling, overtired parents, and kids excited to be out of school for a couple weeks set the stage. There is pressure to enjoy every minute, to be with the ones you love non-stop because you hardly see each other the rest of the year. Bodies are wired on Christmas cookies and coffee. Tempers grow short as no one is sleeping well in their makeshift bed with cousins piled next to them. "It's the Most Wonderful Time of the Year"—or is it?

Many of our expectations and desires with our new relationships are good. It's good to want to have a close-knit, supportive relationship. It's good to want to spend time together as a family. It's good to want to see your grandchildren and be a part of their lives. The problem lies in the fact that our best motives are marred by the brokenness in our hearts and

MAKING ROOM FOR HER

the world. *Good desires easily become unreasonable expectations.* To desire a supportive relationship is a good thing until our selfish demands rule what we say and do. Paul Tripp says it this way, ". . . because of sin, when good things become ruling things, they become bad things."[1]

We might be tempted to use manipulation or guilt trips to have more time with our family. Or maybe we're inclined to selfishly use our in-law to meet our needs while not thinking of theirs—only calling them when we need a babysitter or a helping hand. The sin in our hearts makes us prone to worship the kingdom of self. We think about what would work best for *my* schedule, for *my* family, for *my* bank account. We fall into the pattern of using people to satisfy our own desires, instead of sacrificially serving others.

Thanks be to God that we are not left in that predicament. Because of Jesus's perfect life, death on the cross, and resurrection, those who trust in Him are given the Holy Spirit. We can be thankful that God is always with us, leading us, guiding our every step, and making us different over time.

Psalm 139:23–24 tells us to ask God to search our hearts, to see if there is any sin in our lives. What freedom is ours when we turn from expectations gone bad and trust in our living Lord. Holiday gathering or otherwise, when our expectations go unmet and we feel the anger or resentment rise within us, we can ask God to show us where our good desires went wrong.

No Expectations?

There's a common saying: "He who expects nothing is seldom disappointed."[2] One common piece of advice among marriage counselors is to lower your expectations for your spouse.

Lower expectations lead to less disappointment. Supposedly, this guards us from being hurt or angry. Yet is this a healthy way to view relationships? The same piece of advice could be applied to a mother-in-law and daughter-in-law. "Have low expectations. Don't assume you will have a great relationship. Expect to have problems." While there is some truth in being careful not to have idealistic expectations—and yes, we can all expect sin to create problems sometimes—there also seems to be a danger in assuming the worst.[3]

Before God changed our hearts, we did not have the capacity to show Christlike love in a hard relationship. But as the Spirit of God works in our hearts, anything is possible. Our own stony hearts are softened to give grace to even the most difficult person. The apostle Paul reminds us to put off our former way of life, the old self, and "to put on the new self, the one created according to God's likeness in righteousness and purity of the truth" (Eph. 4:22–24). That verse gives us much hope for our strained relationships. The world swings to extremes, telling us to either expect an unrealistic utopia or expect the absolute worst, but what does God want for us? Instead of "no expectations" or "impossible expectations" we can have *God's* expectations, especially when we start by loving and understanding one another.

How Expectations Begin

We Have Different Upbringings and Different Ways of Showing Love

Jenny shares this experience about one of her first shopping trips with her MIL:

I grew up in a family that showed their love by serving and giving, so as newlyweds who didn't have much money, whenever we would visit my parents, they'd fill our tank with gas, take us shopping for some needs, and we would leave with a little extra cash in our pocket. I felt taken care of! The first time my mother-in-law asked if I wanted to go shopping during a visit, I thought it could be a bonding experience. But it was awkward.

While my mom and I could shop on our own and also together, my mother-in-law wanted to talk the whole time and give me fashion advice. She actually was saying "no" to things I had picked and showing me what she thought I should buy. In order to please her, I chose a pair of khaki pants with pleats that I hated. In fact, when I finally said I might like them, she took them from me and walked right up to the cashier, laying them on the counter.

I assumed she was buying them. But when the cashier said the price, she just stood there. It was so awkward. I finally took out my money and paid too much for a pair of pants I didn't like. I thought it would help our relationship if I just kept my expectations and preferences to myself. I was twenty-two then, but more than twenty years later, our relationship is still in process.

The way Jenny experienced love from her family was through financial help, especially while they were in graduate school and their budget was tight. She assumed her MIL would want to show love to her in the same way on their shopping trip. But her expectations were met with disappointment and frustration when she came home with a pair of pants she didn't like, and less money in her pocket. Jenny took her family's way of showing love and held it out over her MIL.

As for Jenny's MIL, we can imagine she didn't understand the reason for the awkward silence at the cash register. She probably assumed her DIL showed love the same way she did—by simply having an outing together. And, like Jenny, she probably developed that way of showing love from her own family upbringing. Perhaps the way she bonded with her mother wasn't through receiving financial help, but rather through receiving wisdom and advice. And so she, too, took her family's way of showing love and held it out over her DIL. Both women wanted a bonding experience, but their upbringing and ways of showing love shaped their expectations for how the experience would go.

We Have Different Past Hurts

Deborah shares how her difficult relationship with her MIL shaped her relationship with her DIL:

> My MIL had a difficult life. Her husband left her when her children were young, and she was forced to provide for the family and manage life on her own. She relied heavily on the support of my husband, the oldest of her three children. He carried a heavy burden of responsibility, offering physical and emotional support to his mom. When we got married, many of those burdens were transferred to me.

When we got together with my MIL, she spent a lot of time sharing her struggles with me. She needed help in tangible and emotional ways, from doing her income tax to being a sounding board for her current problems. It was hard not to feel overwhelmed with responsibility for her.

When my own son got married, I was determined not to put any weight of responsibility on my DIL. I wanted to give them space in their new marriage, and not cause them to fear the weight of my expectations. I tried to be a good listener and ask lots of questions— rarely sharing personal struggles in my own life.

But I have learned that my DIL feels like I am too distant from the family. She wonders why I am not more eager to see my grandchildren or be involved in their life. I have tried to be respectful of their marriage, but it seems like things backfired. What I thought was being gracious with time and expectations was received as not caring enough.

Deborah's past hurt intensified her desire for a good relationship with her daughter-in-law. She assumed that if she gave her son and DIL ample space, and took an interest in their lives, they would enjoy a common bond. She expected her DIL to want lots of distance. What she didn't expect was for her daughter-in-law to misinterpret her love. Her hopes and efforts were met with confusion and regret. What were

Deborah's daughter-in-law's past hurts? Did she have some painful experiences in her history too? Our past hurts shape our expectations.

We Have Different Resources (time, money, energy)

Abby's family was on a tight budget. With five kids and limited vacation time, traveling to the other side of the country to see her husband's parents didn't seem realistic. The funds weren't there to cover airfare for the entire family. They preferred a quiet, low-stress getaway with their family and found comfort in the tradition of a yearly stay at a lakeside cabin. The familiar journey to Abby's parents was also relaxing—like going home. It felt comfortable to go where they all knew they could just be themselves. Besides, Abby's parents thrived on these consistent visits. And the distance was far shorter.

Judy, Abby's mother-in-law, thinks about this differently. She wonders why so little effort is made to visit them. Judy accepts Abby's close relationship to her mother. But it is hard not to resent the more frequent visits made to the other grandparents. Judy's job responsibilities keep them from going to visit more often and she regrets not knowing her grandchildren better. With some creativity and savings, Judy and her husband make plans for a yearly visit from their grandchildren.

Both Abby and Judy don't understand each other's point of view. Both have the good desire to spend time together. But limited time and money keep that from happening regularly. What are Abby desires? What are Judy's hopes? How have their unmet expectations impacted their relationship? Our time, money and energy impact the expectations we have for ourselves and for our in-law.

A Better Dream

When I (Stacy) felt like family togetherness on our vacation was smothering, I needed to remember that Barb desired this out of a heart of love. She wanted to make the most of our time together as a family. I also needed to adjust my idea of how much "rest and relaxation" would be possible during a vacation with thirteen people. It helps to talk openly and honestly with each another. My in-laws generously provided for the vacation, so we didn't want to seem selfish or ungrateful by not going along with their plans. Yet how much frustration could have been avoided if expectations for togetherness were talked through beforehand?

What have I (Barb) learned about loving my daughter-in-law well? When frustrations arise over unmet expectations, I need to remember that we both love each other. All of our expectations arise out of good intentions, and usually, any difference we have can be traced back to the things we mentioned before—having different upbringings, ways of showing love, past hurts, or resources. A simple but practical idea is to ask before I plan. Now, before I get a script in my head, I'll explore with Stacy and my other grown children what their expectations are for our time together. How can we allow flex time for families to do whatever they call fun? What about encouraging couples to have a much-needed evening out while we stay with the grandchildren? Dinner on us.

Here's something we've learned over time: more than we are displaying our love for our in-law to one another, we are ultimately displaying God's love for them. And what does God's love look like? It looks sacrificial. It looks like Jesus, who seeks to serve instead of be served (Mark 10:45). And as we fight to follow his example, he fills us with his grace, humility, and forgiving love so that we can get the job done. He helps us remember that true humility does not demand its own way but considers others (Phil. 2:3–4). If the desire to be heard and respected has driven a wedge in your relationship, be on your guard against comparison and competition and remember that to serve is not to harshly manage or direct. To serve is to tenderly come alongside and assist, the focus being on the good of the other person, not ourselves. Or, said succinctly, serving your in-law in a Christlike way means focusing on "*she*, not *me*." Can you imagine how much healthier the relationship would be if both parties approached things this way? It certainly would have helped our past family vacations!

One way to put this servanthood into practice and get better at the "she, not me" mentality is to become a student of our mother-in-law or daughter-in-law. When we do this, it forces our focus off of ourselves and what makes *us* happiest, and gives us eyes to see what makes *her* most happy. Ask God to show you the best way to love her. When do her eyes light up with appreciation? When you offer to do the dishes? If you give her something chocolate? How about an offer to watch the kids so she and your son can enjoy a date night? A note of appreciation or a text to let her know of your prayers could mean the most. If you still don't know—ask! Showing Jesus's servant-hearted love to your mother-in-law or daughter-in-law will fill you and your family with joy.

Here's something else we can remember—our family is not the problem. The problem is not your mother-in-law or daughter-in-law. Sin is the problem. Sin makes every relationship hard, and it's in every one of our hearts, wreaking all sorts of havoc. So do we throw our hands up in the air and give up planning time together? No. Why? Because God created relationships to help us see what his real love looks like. And your relationship with your mother-in-law or daughter-in-law is no exception. It is designed to not only show you what God's love for you looks like, but also embody that kind of love to your in-law. If you give up now, you'll miss out on a chance to not only know him better, but become more like him.

God lavishes his love on us (1 John 3:1–3). He shows us his love not because of what we do, but simply out of love. In love, God willing sacrificed his own Son. In love, the Son suffered a cruel death on the cross for us (Isa. 53:5–6). Our performance is not what made him love us; in fact, that we would even try to perform for his love is one of the things he died for! Yet even in our sin and failures, he set his love on us anyway and chose to serve us, die for us, and make us new. If this is the way he has loved us, why would we turn around to others, including our in-law, and keep refining the script for the perfect performance? Nothing will separate us from God's love (Rom. 8:38–39). When we get our eyes off our expectations and onto God, his faithful love reveals how selfish our plans and demands for others can be.

Our mother-in-law, daughter-in-law relationships are an invitation from God to enjoy his love. Is your relationship hard? Have you experienced hurt feelings from unmet expectations? Sinful selfishness can be found in us all. How might remembering God's sacrificial love to you rewrite your expectations? God calls us to extend the love he has shown to us to the precious woman we call mother-in-law or daughter-in-law. God is the true director of the drama. He knows you intimately and provides generously for all your needs (Rom. 8:32). His love orchestrates all things for your good (Rom. 8:28–29). Let that love fuel you. Enjoy it for yourself, and then let it overflow onto her.

What God Equips Us to Do

Sometimes it's easy to consider our in-law as an exception to the rules of biblical wisdom. We'll apply certain passages to every other relationship but this one. We'll follow the Bible's instructions when it comes to our kids, or our church relationships, or our work friends, and so on. But when an in-law gets thrown in the mix, all that scriptural guidance gets thrown out. We think, "It's not worth it—after all, we only see them a couple times a year!" Or "It's too painful; there's no way God could be asking me to do that with *her*." To fight our tendency of applying God's Word selectively, another helpful way to develop a Christlike heart toward your in-law is to recall various passages about loving others—passages you already know and agree with in a general sense—and apply them directly to your MIL or DIL. We aren't off the hook with these when it comes to our in-law, and we find when we implement them with her, we grow in Christlikeness.

Appreciate Your In-Law for Who God Created Her to Be

"God created man in his own image" (Gen. 1:27). You likely know that passage. You probably believe he ordained the number of hairs on our head and the number of our days on this earth (Ps. 139:16). You already know he creates each image-bearer with unique gifts, abilities, and personalities. God's expectations for us are rooted in love and meant to produce fruitful relationships on earth. So consider this: your in-law was purposefully created to be the mother of your husband, or the wife of your son. It was no accident. If you believe these things in a general sense, you must believe it about her. After all, wouldn't you want her to believe these things about you?

Many of us have an ideal image in our mind, the kind of person we expect for a MIL or DIL. It's the person that we prayed for, perhaps created in our image. Yet it's not our choice. When we marry, or when our sons marry, we are given the package deal. If we hold onto our expectation of who our in-law is supposed to be, we'll likely be disappointed or resentful. Instead, we need to thank God for the unique person that they are and ask him to help us love them just as they are. After all, God loved us when we were still his enemies. Shouldn't we extend the same grace to our in-law? God made us unique and wrote an intentional story for our lives. Shouldn't we treat our in-law like we believe the same about her story? And if we don't, what does that say about our belief in the God who made her?

Love Your In-Law as Yourself

Jesus gave us the greatest commandment when he said, "Love the Lord your God with all your heart, with all your soul, and with all your mind" (Matt. 22:37). This was followed by the second greatest commandment: "Love your neighbor as yourself" (Matt. 22:39). Is your neighbor only the person living in the house next door to you? Of course not. Your neighbor is anyone in your sphere of contact and influence. Your in-law is your neighbor, and we are to love them as we love ourselves. This passage applies to her too!

It is natural to look out for yourself. We all reflexively go about our days ensuring we are comfortable, with enough food and clothing, with an eye toward our preferences being honored. But it is harder to do that for someone else. If we are to love our in-law as ourselves, we should be willing to look out for their well-being. How can we make them feel loved and cared for? What are their preferences with food or time or schedules?

Show Honor to Your In-Law

Exodus 20:12 tells us we should honor our father and mother, that our days may be long in the land. We'd agree that this biblical principle should apply to every Christian family. So why not ours? We'd want our kids to follow this wisdom, so why would we not want to follow it ourselves when it comes to our in-law? Even though your MIL is not your biological parent, she is the mom of your husband. And since we are one with our husband, she should be honored just as our own mother.

First Peter 2:17 reminds us to show honor to all people, which includes our in-law. This verse doesn't give an exemption clause if your in-law is difficult to get along with. We show honor by praying for them, listening to them, and caring for their needs.

Or consider Philippians 2, which exhorts us to consider others as more important than ourselves. Just as Christ humbled himself to the point of death on a cross, so we are to humble ourselves in the service of others. Peter and Paul's aim in sharing these principles was not so they might be printed in a book and left on a shelf—no, their aim was for these principles to drill down into our everyday relationships, including our MIL or DIL. So we must ask ourselves: how can we love our in-law through serving them sacrificially? How might we, even when things are inconvenient, lay aside our preferences for the sake of gospel love?

Live Peaceably with Your In-Law

Romans 12:18 reminds us that we're to live peaceably with all, *as far as it depends on us.* God recognizes that relationships are two-way streets. We don't have control over others, but we do have control over our own actions and attitudes. In other words, she may not choose to live peaceably with us in certain moments, but regardless of her heart or behavior, we will choose to apply this passage in *our* heart and behavior, making an effort to live peaceably. Why? Because more than we owe that to her, we owe it to God. He's asked us to live this way with everyone. The good news is that he can help us obey through his Spirit. We can ask God to help us exercise control over our tongues and our tempers, especially when expectations are dashed, and he really will give us the ability to do so. We can be quick to give grace and assume the best of our in-law's intentions, even when feelings have been hurt, because the Lord in us is helping us be at peace in our relationship, moving toward our in-law in love and grace.

What We Can Expect from God

Life will not always go as expected. Only some of our expectations are reasonable, and as we grow, we learn how to identify those that are unreasonable. Sometimes that journey feels like a guessing game when it comes to other humans, but here's something wonderful: God does not leave us guessing. In the Bible, God tells us what his expectations are for our life. And God invites us to have expectations of him—he tells us what we can count on.

What is unreasonable to expect from any human relationship, we can expect God to give us—love that does not change or fail. At times, relationships hurt, but nothing will ever cause God to change his mind and withdraw his love from his children. Jesus's life tells us God knows the worst about us and never stops loving us. In Jesus, God invites us to expect a loving relationship with himself—forever (John 3:16). He gave his Son to die for you to invite you to a never-ending holy and happy friendship with himself (Rom. 8:38–39). In short, *expect God to love you*. No matter what. No matter who your in-law is, no matter how rough things may be, no matter who might be failing you—God will meet you, love you, and fill you up. He will never fail that expectation.

Want to know something else God wants us to expect of him? That he doesn't leave us as we are (Phil. 1:6). This means that as a child of God, you're not caught in a rut. God's transforming work through his Spirit and Word renews our minds (Rom. 12:2). True, you can expect uncomfortable or challenging times in your mother-in-law or daughter-in-law relationship. A truth greater yet—you can expect trouble. Yet, we do not have to fear the hard times as if they will destroy us. In God's hands, troubles are instruments to change and grow you into the woman he created you to be (Rom. 5:3–5; 8:28–29; 2 Cor. 3:18; Col. 3:10).

Set your expectations on God's promises of unfailing love, rich mercy, transformative power, and assured hope. You will never be disappointed. ✔

Discussion Questions

1. For Barb and Stacy, expectations seem to reveal themselves during holiday gatherings. What about you? What situations tend to reveal your expectations of your in-law?

2. What general expectations do you have for your relationship with your in-law? Where do you think those expectations came from?

3. When you are not walking in step with the Spirit, how do you typically handle those unmet expectations? (Retaliation, cold shoulder, screaming, withdrawal, bitterness, etc.)

4. Examine your own heart as you consider your answer to the previous question. Why do you think you resort to these kinds of reactions? What do you think this response will gain you?

5. Remember that God equips us to love our in-law through the power of his Holy Spirit. Consider the four principles listed in this chapter—the ones that we sometimes forget to specifically apply to our MIL or DIL. Which of these challenges you most? Why?

6. What encourages you most regarding what we can expect from God? Why?

7. Do you lean more toward idealistic expectations of your in-law, or toward expecting the worst? How has this kept you from pursuing God's love and hope in your in-law relationship?

COMMUNICATING
WELL

Building Your Relationship One Step at a Time

I t was an exciting time in life. Ben and I (Stacy) had just been married. We returned to Michigan for our wedding during Christmas break, just weeks before I began student teaching. After our New Orleans honeymoon (don't judge us—it was cheap and warm!), we came back to my parents' house to pack up my childhood bedroom and load the U-Haul. It was a family affair.

Ben and I both grew up in the same town. His family lived about a ten-minute bike ride away. On a chilly January morning our families gathered for one final breakfast together before we loaded the truck and moved twelve hours to the arctic tundra of Minnesota. As it turned out, Barb and Ron were also preparing to move. They were clearing out their own house in preparation for a move to South Africa where they would begin a new ministry. Lucky for us, they needed to find a home for all of their furniture. With only wedding money and a plethora of new Christmas ornaments to our name, we gladly accepted the gift of hand-me-down couches, tables, and beds for our new apartment. Both our dads worked tirelessly as we loaded things in record time. Just as we prepared to close the U-Haul, we got a call from Barb. "Um . . . I think you left the china cabinet at our house." Oops—one more trip still had to be made!

In all of the hustle and bustle of the wedding, two families moving and starting a new life together, communication with our parents wasn't something that Ben and I had given much thought to. (Keep in mind this was the era before cell phones, FaceTime, text messages, and a host of other ways that we now use to communicate.) We knew that Barb and Ron would likely return to the states in about two years for furlough. In the meantime, we saved our pennies in hopes of going to visit them before any babies arrived on the scene. I loved Barb and Ron and naively had no worries about communication and building a relationship with them. We were happy to see them follow God's call on their lives to an overseas ministry. But living thousands of miles away has ramifications, and things were not as easy as I expected.

During the first few years Barb and Ron were overseas, we moved three times, finished a church internship in Minnesota, began my first real teaching job, moved to Kentucky for seminary, and became pregnant with our firstborn daughter. By a small miracle we saved enough money to travel to South Africa for an extended visit. We had a special time together, but a few weeks doesn't make up for over a year without seeing one another.

Things felt awkward and jerky. There was so much that had happened in both our lives during our time apart—where did we begin trying to catch up? Although everyone was excited to see each other, our interactions weren't as natural as I had envisioned. At first conversations were surfacy, guarded from any real heart issues we were facing. It became clear that the lack of communication up till now was bearing unripe fruit: we didn't really know each other—not in these new roles, in this new season. And it's hard to develop biblical love for those you don't really know. Communication was more difficult than we assumed it would be, and slowed the growth of our new relationship.

In hindsight, I wish I would have been more intentional in communicating with Barb. It can be hard for a newly married wife to see the value of building a good relationship with her mother-in-law. I was so focused on creating *my* new family that in-laws, especially living across the ocean, were far from my mind. Why is communication important in building a positive relationship with your mother-in-law or daughter-in-law? And how is it possible? Especially when you're far away?

Communication for the Purpose of Communion

Few daughters-in-law and mothers-in-law would choose one another as their ideal friend. It is no easy thing to become a member of a different family! Not everyone is going to want to have a deep bond at first. Yet in-law relationships can have great value. God intends extended families to love and help each other. Don't be discouraged if you begin on a superficial level. Keep God's goal for your family in mind, and start small. Deep bonds don't happen overnight. Life happens. Personal crises are opportunities to grow your family together (Gal. 6:2). Don't expect the in-law relationship to be ideal overnight! A deeper, more loving communion is the result of intentional communication over a long period of time.

From our first conversation Stacy and I (Barb) knew—we are joyfully different. I process my feelings internally. Stacy processes her feelings verbally. Differences are normal. God did not create us as clones. He creates individuals. Each one unique. How can we expect someone to fit into our mold? Stacy and I have learned not only to expect but to enjoy each other's personalities and communication styles, even though these differences can lead to misunderstandings.

If you want to develop healthy communication with your in-law, the best thing to try at the starting line is to slow down and listen to yourself. Sometimes in the swirl of emotions, hormones, and sin, we miss what our words tell us about ourselves. Listen to what your words tell you about your heart. We may say, "Oh I didn't mean that." But Jesus says that our words are simply the overflow of our hearts (Matt. 12:34).

So, take inventory of your words, and let them reveal what's going on in your heart. Consider the ways you speak to your in-law. Stop and ask, "Is my way of talking with my in-law ultimately for my benefit? To make me look better, to justify my actions, to win the argument, to earn love and respect?" Or perhaps this: "Do I seriously desire to love her because of how Jesus has loved me?[1] Do I want God to use my words for his loving purpose in her life?"

Another way to develop healthy communication is to stop and remember the reason God gave us the gift of communication to begin with. God's purpose for our communication is *communion*. God is the great communicator. He speaks to us because he wants to enjoy relationship with us, and his Words to us reveal his heart. We are made in God's image, which means that we too are communicators. Just as God speaks to us through his Word in order to build a relationship, so we use our words to commune with others. Communion is defined as an "act or instance of sharing or intimate fellowship."[2] Would you say this is your aim when speaking to your in-law? If not, what is?

How can we make communion with one another our priority? Stacy and I are learning to use our words to "bear each other's burdens." When either of us has a crazy week, we ask each other for prayer. When I hesitate to interrupt her demanding schedule with my requests, I remember what communion means. What might communion look like for you and your in-law? How can your words help lighten her load or create a moment of safety and intimacy?

But *She* Should Be the One Initiating!

Bill and Janice were thrilled that their son, Jason, had found a wonderful, godly woman to spend his life with. They had prayed for Jason's future wife from the time that he was a little boy. It was exciting to watch God's plan unfold as their long-awaited prayer was answered. Amy was sweet, motivated, and seemed to complement Jason well. Janice had high hopes of a close daughter-like relationship with Amy. But as time went on, the fairy-tale family life that she planned in her mind didn't seem to happen. Jason and Amy moved across the country and rarely came to visit. Busy work schedules and a young family made traveling daunting. Phone calls seldom happened, with most communication happening through short texts, in abbreviations that Bill and Janice weren't familiar with (what is IDK anyway?). Janice couldn't help but feel disappointed and left out of her son and daughter-in-law's life. And to add to the sting, it seemed like Jason and Amy unfairly spent more time with the other side of the family. Janice didn't want to be a burden through calling or asking for visits, so she mainly kept to herself and tried to be content with their yearly summer gathering.

Jason and Amy felt like they were barely keeping their heads above water. With bustling careers and three children under six, their main goal was survival. Amy was focused on the basics: full bellies, clean clothes, and getting to work on time. She wished her in-laws were closer to provide more hands-on support, yet also knew that communication with her mother-in-law needed improvement. She barely had time to call anyone during the week. How could she find time to reach out to Janice too? It seemed like the only time they talked was when Jason got around to scheduling a family Zoom call (which wasn't very often). She wondered why Janice and Bill didn't initiate calling more often? Amy knew they were still working part-time and had an active life in their church body. But didn't they want to invest in their grandchildren more? Or come visit more than once each year? She wrestled with her own feelings of hurt and disappointment. *We need help in this season. Where are they?*

Do any of these things sounds familiar? If you're a mother-in-law, maybe you commiserate with Janice. On one hand you're happy for your son's full life. On the other hand, you may wish your daughter-in-law showed more interest in getting to know you. It's hard to know the right balance between showing love for your family through communication and being overbearing. Janice was well aware of the "monster-in-law" stereotype, and she was determined not to fall into the same pattern. She erred on the side of being less involved than overinvolved. Plus, it seemed fitting that the younger generation should be the one to initiate conversation. The kids led such a busy life, she would wait for them to find a time that worked in their schedule to talk.

Ironically, Amy viewed Janice's lack of phone calls and visits as a disinterest in their family. It was hard not to compare the amount of time her in-law's spent with their daughter's family who lived nearby. She admired many things about Janice and wished that she had a closer relationship with her. But it felt like a burden to be the one always expected to initiate communication. Surely Bill and Janice had more free time—all of their children were out of the nest. Why did they so seldom call or visit? She had a sinking feeling that Bill and Janice were disappointed in her, even if the words never came out of their mouths.

Do you see the problem? Both parties think that the other should be initiating communication. And it leaves both mother-in-law and daughter-in-law disappointed. Both are fixated on the speck in someone else's eye without first taking out the log in their own (Matt. 7:5). Both Janice and Amy are claiming their rights, assuming they're getting the short end of the stick. The mother-in-law has more time, so *she* should be the primary one to initiate calls. The daughter-in-law is so busy, so *she* should be the one to put calls or visits on the calendar. But the way of humility looks to serve the other person, whether or not your expectations are fulfilled. Sadly, when each woman is focused on what the other should be doing, they both lose out on getting to know each other. Amy and Janice's lack of communication (as assumptions about communication) caused misunderstanding and hurt feelings to permeate their relationship.

Both Janice and Amy would be wise to consider the pattern Jesus sets before us. He doesn't only converse with those who deserve it, with those who follow all the religious laws. In John 4 we see him crossing the lines of both race and sex, as he talks with the Samaritan woman at the well. Normally Jews would never talk with Samaritans. They were considered unclean, unworthy to be spoken to. In addition, speaking to a woman in a public sphere was also a rarity. Even his disciples "were amazed that he was talking with a woman" (John 4:27). Not to mention a woman who was living a life of adultery (John 4:16–18). But Jesus's concern for the woman's soul made cultural rules irrelevant. He purposefully pursued someone who didn't deserve it! The hope of the gospel is for everyone, and no one is beyond the grace of God.

Maybe you feel like your in-law doesn't deserve to be pursued by you. Maybe she's hurt you through critical words, or slander, or neglect. But God calls us to move toward those who don't deserve our love, to cover over their hurtful offenses with love (1 Pet. 4:8). We extend the grace God gives us, initiating conversation even when it's hard.

It's easy to get trapped in a spiral of self-pity, to feel like your needs are being neglected or overlooked. Instead we need to follow the servant-hearted example of Christ, who lifted his eyes from his own troubles in order to serve others. Think of Jesus on the cross asking John to care for his mom. What if our focus was serving our in-law instead of counting the ways we feel wounded? Love is patient, kind, and keeps no record of wrongs (1 Cor. 13:4–7). So put away the scoreboard of who called who last. Be the first to initiate a conversation and begin to rebuild what's been lost.

The Value and Fruit of Flexibility.

But how do you initiate a conversation? When it comes to communication, there can be a real issue with the generation gap. Mothers-in-law may prefer face-to-face conversations or phone calls where they can hear their daughter-in-law's voice and tone. A lot can be miscommunicated when you only see words on a screen. Not to mention texts and emails can seem so impersonal! But many daughters-in-law might prefer the ease and efficiency of text messages or email. A quick message can be sent when they have a break at work or in the moments waiting in the carpool line. Unscheduled or long phone calls can feel intrusive to their busy day.

Have you noticed how your MIL or DIL likes to communicate? Even if it's not your preference, look for ways to reach out to her that align with her real life. If you aren't close enough to see it yourself, then go a step further and *ask* her what her favorite mode of communication is. For both parties, this is another opportunity to lay down our "rights" and show deference and honor to the other.

Flexibility is defined as bending easily without breaking. The only constant in our life is God. He will never change. But practically everything else around us does change![3] We need to be flexible in many areas of life: our schedules, our parenting, our food choices, our budget, just to name a few. Being willing to be flexible with our means of communication helps us keep a humble perspective, not insisting on our way but following the way of the cross. Bending to accommodate your in-law's preferences demonstrates a kind and gentle spirit—the kind of spirit Christ has (Matt. 11:29). Can you imagine what would happen if *both* of you were trying to show love to one another when it came to communication, "outdoing each other in showing honor" (Rom. 12:10 ESV)? Hearts would be softened and offenses might be more easily overlooked. You might even learn something new, like what the latest abbreviations mean while texting—or that picking up the phone to call not only didn't kill you, but offered an unexpectedly refreshing conversation!

As it turns out, if we stay flexible in communication, the generational differences can bear fruit as both sides lean toward each other instead of away. One can be brought a bit more up to speed, the other can enjoy a few more opportunities to take a breath and slow down.

Learning to be flexible and adaptable with our means of communication will help break down barriers between generations. Kids can give us a whole new reason to connect. Living hundreds of miles away from my (Stacy) in-laws has forced us to find creative ways to share our life with them. We've used FaceTime and Zoom calls to include Barb and Ron in a piano recital or just to see our daughter's latest gymnastic move. As our kids have entered the teenage years, they have access to devices that allow them to connect on their own with their grandparents. Sometimes it can be hard to schedule a time when everyone can get on the phone to say hi, but Barb has often reached out to them individually, connecting with them after school or when they have free time on the weekend.

One other creative idea to consider as you seek to build better communication throughout your greater family is a virtual "drop in." This is something that Barb and Ron recently planned for our extended family after a long stretch of radio silence because of COVID-19. It had been months since we all connected; even an entire year. So Barb and Ron organized a drop-in family Zoom call for our extended family. They opened the call for a span of two hours in the afternoon, inviting family members to jump on and say hi as their schedule allowed. It was a great tool that allowed Barb and Ron to catch up with each family in a way that worked with everyone's busy Saturday schedule. Sometimes fighting for good communication means being willing to think outside the box, especially when distance doesn't allow for many in-person visits.

In all these ways and more, when we fight to be flexible, we'll see the fruit!

Love Your Husband by Loving Your In-Law: How Communication Affects Your Marriage

Whether you just married the man of your dreams or you've been married to him for three decades, a healthy marriage results in learning how to show love to one another. You both delight in the physical affection of one another and look for ways to bring a smile to each other's face. Maybe he joins your favorite activity or you cook him his favorite meal. You spend time together and talk through your hopes, dreams, and fears. One of the things that brings both Stacy and Barb the most joy is seeing our own marriages in a season of health. But for many couples, the closest family relationships can either strengthen the marriage or strain it. How does our relationship with our in-law affect our marriage?

Chloe and Brett have been married only two short years. They've been intentional from the get-go about building a great marriage. They went to pre-marriage counseling, read marriage books together, and even attended a weekend marriage retreat. Chloe loves finding new ways to show her husband love, like surprising him with tickets to his favorite team's football game. Yet one constant source of tension in their relationship is with Brett's mom. "I feel so drained after being with your mom for the holidays. She talks incessantly, and never bothers to ask me any questions. Doesn't she care about how my life is going? I feel like I can never get a word in."

Over time, Chloe voices her complaints to Brett on repeat. Brett loves his mom, and while he realizes she's more on the talker side of things than the listener, she's not committing any crimes. Chloe's complaints about Brett's mom are starting to grate on him. Every time he hears his wife griping about his mom, he starts to feel tense. How can he appease his wife while not hurting his mom? How do you ask someone you love to stop being who they are?

The communication issues between Chloe and Brett's mom have not only created relational problems for the two of them, but have also caused emotional stress for Brett and Chloe in their marriage. Brett feels caught in the middle between two women he deeply loves and respects.

One thing few marriage books mention is the impact your relationship with your in-laws has on your spouse. Think about the dynamics of this relationship and why it can so easily affect our emotions.

"There are good reasons for why in-laws trigger us so easily. First, all long-term relationships harbor trigger potential. Casual, noncommitted relationships just don't go where it hurts. Quite frankly, not that many people care as deeply about what you do and do not do as your in-laws.

Second, the in-law family is often the second closest we have, right after our family of origin."[4]

We can get easily annoyed with our in-law when we feel like they're overstepping their bounds, excluding us, or showing favoritism. Though our friendships can wound us in other ways, they aren't likely to have strong opinions on how we use our vacation time or who will host the annual Christmas gathering. But our families do care. When the relationship is deeper and connects multiple people in the family, there's more potential for hurt. More relationships are at stake. In addition, the pull of our blood relatives is stronger than most other relationships. The desire to appease both sides runs high.

If we are a daughter-in-law, one of the best things we can do to strengthen our marriage is to build a good relationship with our in-law. Or, put more succinctly, we can love our husband by loving his mom. If we are proactive here instead of reactive, our marriage is more likely to flourish. With good communication we learn to ask questions, to listen with empathy, and then find practical ways to show our care. Dr. Juli Slattery from Focus on the Family encourages us, "Ultimately, fostering a healthy relationship with your mother-in-law is an expression of your love for your husband and your commitment to living out the love of Christ. You never know . . . you just might make a friend in the process."[5]

On the other hand, hearing constant complaints about his mother will wear down the resolve of any husband and can easily result in anger or withdrawal. In other words, it's not just your communication with *her* that matters, it's your communication with *him* too. And the reverse is true as well. A mother-in-law who complains to her son about her daughter-in-law will add friction to his marriage. She must not only pursue the practice of Christlike speech with her DIL, but with her son as well. It's worth putting in the time and effort, communicating through both our words and actions, to build a healthy in-law relationship.

Any relationship is going to have its ups and downs. And when your in-law seems very different than yourself, it can be easy to throw in the towel, leaving all communication up to your husband or son.

Now's the time to ask, "Am I willing to see my in-law relationship as an opportunity to grow?" "Am I considering how my words might impact the marriage as a whole?" "Am I pursuing healthy communication not only with her, but with him?" You can depend on your heavenly Father to help you value your in-law. He will lead you into your new role as either daughter-in-law or mother-in-law with a sense of joy and purpose—that you become more like his Son. As a mother-in-law, you will learn to love your son in a new way—by loving his wife. And as a daughter-in-law, you will learn to love your husband in a new way—by loving his mother.[6] When both parties approach communication this way, marriages are far healthier and wedges are far fewer.

Communicating Difficult Conversations with Your In-law

Here's an alarming statistic: three out of four couples have significant problems with their in-laws.[7] If that is you, take heart that you're not alone. This is an often difficult and tricky relationship to navigate. But we don't need to lose hope and assume things will never get better. When the Spirit of God is at work in your heart, change is possible. God's Word reminds us, "Therefore, if anyone is in Christ, he is a new creation; the old has passed away, and see, the new has come!" (2 Cor. 5:17).

We can ask the Spirit of God to give us patience, kindness, and compassion for our in-law, even when interacting with her is difficult. When we commit to praying for our in-law, our hearts will inevitably soften. Maybe the change will be more in your life than your in-law's, but you can rest assured that God will not waste any family trials that you're experiencing.

A Note to Daughters-in-Law

Maybe you're reading this book, searching for some nugget of wisdom that will help you move forward in a strained relationship with your mother-in-law. While there are no easy, black-and-white answers, here are three simple and helpful steps to communicate well during conflict with your mother-in-law . . .

1. Respectfully share your concerns with your husband. It's easy to voice our complaints with a whiny and demanding spirit. We feel entitled to be treated better than we are. Yet our bad attitudes might push our biggest ally further away. After all, this is the woman who gave your husband life, cared for him for two decades, and sacrificed much of her time and resources. It can be hurtful for your husband to hear his mother berated.

Look for ways to gently share with your husband your concerns about your mother-in-law, while also affirming all the things you appreciate about her. Let your attitude be, "How can we strive for peace and unity in the family?" instead of "Let me tell you what your mother did this time!" There may be a very real issue you need to discuss with him about her, but the posture you take and the attitude you bring to the conversation communicates just as much as your words do. Think of it this way: If two people were having a hard conversation about your legitimate flaws—and we all have flaws—how would you want them to handle it? You wouldn't want them to talk in a way that tears you down, but one that addresses the issue for the sake of building up or restoring something broken. You'd want them to see not just the bad, but the good too. You'd want gentleness. You'd want the facts to be considered in context. You wouldn't want to sound like a gossip session where the conversation relished your failure or scoffed in self-righteousness at your mistakes. You'd want the tone to be warm and respectful, with the aim of mending what went wrong. If that's what you'd want when it comes to your own flaws and failures, extend the same courtesy to your in-law.

2. *Allow your husband to initiate the conversation with your mother-in-law.* As close as you might be to your mother-in-law, your husband is closer. The family ties that bind can cause a parent to have a natural soft spot for their own child. If you're having any delicate conversations with your mother-in-law, from changing vacation plans to discussing a disagreement, it

may be better received by her son.[8] Allow your husband to lead in your marriage by initiating the hard conversations with his parents. It doesn't mean that you can't be involved or share your own perspective. But let the main feedback come from him. And the reverse is true as well. If the problem in your family is with your parents, most of the time, you should be the one to talk with them about it. There are exceptions, of course, but the goal is to frame complicated conversations in a way that will be best received by all parties.

3. Humbly receive any feedback that is offered. Rarely does a hard conversation end without complaints and concerns expressed on both sides. How might you have contributed to the tension in the relationship? Ask God to prepare your heart for any critical feedback that you might receive. Try to put yourself in your mother-in-law's shoes. Why might she be responding the way she is? Is there added stress in her life—maybe she is caring for aging parents or she's getting tired in a difficult job? Be ready to offer compassion, forgiveness, and a willingness to own up to whatever part you may have played in what's happened. Biblical confrontation requires not only courage and conviction, but correctability.

A Note to Mothers-in-Law

1. Talk to God and your husband about your concerns. You may feel hurt by what your daughter-in-law said, but before you approach her with angry accusations, do some inner work. Ask God to show you the truth about your heart. Love your husband well—ask for his insight. Let him know his perspective is valued. And as you go to him, choose your words carefully. Don't put him in the awkward position of having to take sides. A divisive stance will not move your family toward unity. Rather, approach the conversation with the goal of love and restoration for your family. Think of it this way: if your DIL and son were having a similar conversation, how would you want them to handle it? With love and respect and an aim to mend the division, of course. You wouldn't want them to drag your name through the mud or approach the conversation with malicious tones. You'd want them to believe the best and talk it through in a spirit of gentleness, not a spirit of gossip or bitterness. So, in your own conversation with your husband, extend the courtesy you'd want.

2. *Talk to your daughter-in-law with love and respect.* Nurturing family relationships is well worth the prayerful effort. Love and respect for your daughter-in-law are the foundation of a nurturing relationship. You will not force your daughter-in-law to change. Invite her to share the thoughts and feelings that prompted her words and actions. Ask good questions to show your sincere interest and clarify your misconceptions. Resist a defensive posture that only leads to an argument. Share your perspective without accusations. Your goal is not to "win," but to nurture.

3. *Refrain from talk about your daughter-in-law's marital issues.* A close relationship with your daughter-in-law may open the door to off-limits topics. You are not a marital counselor. If you hear about your son's behavior, it can be hurtful and confusing. You are not in a position of defending your son or counseling him. How will your son feel to know that his mother and wife have discussed their sexual intimacy or latest private argument? He will feel betrayed by his wife. (This does not mean that you should abandon your daughter-in-law's cry for help in an abusive situation, however. In the case of abuse disclosure, ensure her physical safety, learn what the reporting laws in your state require of you, and suggest a counselor.) Remember your role—to encourage your son and daughter-in-law's marriage.

Their marriage will survive and thrive as they share personal information, not with you, but with each other.

Communing with Your In-law

Women serving as a MIL or DIL can expect this new (or not so new!) role to bring both joy and challenge. There's a delicate balance to achieve as women desire to fulfill their God-ordained role in serving and yet influencing, the other. Consider these ways to nurture communication:

1. Communicate that you are on the same team

Let each other know you are cheering them on. Show your support through affirming words and actions to back them up.

2. Speak graciously and biblically

Come alongside your in-law with prayer and practical help. Ask God to open the way for you to study God's Word together! Look for ways to speak of God—his Person and work—in your mind and heart.

3. Live with integrity

Refuse to listen to or engage in negative, belittling conversations aimed at your in-law. Be known as one who speaks gracious, affirming words that respect her role as wife or mother. Even if she has hurt your feelings or disappointed you, you can still obey what the Bible says about godly speech. Even in hard conversations when you need to address an issue directly, you can still do so in gentleness and respect.

4. Encourage

Even if she is distant or difficult, look for ways to credit and bless her. Stay faithful. Care enough to pray for her and the entire family. Communicate your gratitude for her sacrificial service. Just as you would want done for you, be quick to notice the good she's doing instead of the bad.

5. Discuss the calendar in advance

Make certain that you communicate collaboratively about family events. Discuss holiday celebrations and come to a mutual decision. Sync activities with each other's family calendars. Stand firm to your commitments. Promote the other's objectives as vigorously as you promote your own.

6. Speak up

Make sure your in-law stays informed of developments affecting your life. Speak into the unique issues you face, without intercepting her role. Ensure that she doesn't get caught off guard by being unaware. Offer insights from your viewpoint. Ask for her opinion.

7. Model gratitude

Your in-law may or may not have had a good example of a loving MIL/DIL relationship. Set the example of how to love and show thanks. Words of affirmation and gratitude, showing interest in what interests her, and being an active listener in conversations can affirm your in-law's role in your family.

8. Believe the Best

There will be times when you feel misunderstood or maligned even by the most caring in-law. Remember the concerns and challenges she carries and choose to believe the absolute best of her character. Our great, loving God can be trusted to care for your family, despite the frailties of both mother-in-law and daughter-in-law.

Conclusion

Good communication unlocks relationships, allowing them to flourish. When Jesus calls us to communion, it is not just for us. Jesus has an even greater purpose: that the world will know God.

> "I have given them the glory you have given me, so that they may be one as we are one. I am in them and you are in me, so that they may be made completely one, that the world may know you have sent me and have loved them as you have loved me." (John 17:22–23)

Just think. As believers in Christ, our in-law relationships communicate the beauty of God's love to the watching world. And even if our in-law is not a believer, our Christlike ministry to them also paints a picture of the gospel to the world around us. To our children. To the generations to come. To neighbors. To friends. Impossible? Yes! Our best behavior will not transform the hearts of the world around us. Yet as God leads our needy souls to rest in his all-sufficient power, he supplies the unity we need. Listen to him. Talk to him. Ask him to reach the world for Christ through your in-law relationship. ✍

Discussion Questions

1. How do you normally communicate with your in-laws?

2. What can you learn about initiating conversations from Jesus's dialogue with the woman at the well (John 4)? What cultural divides did he cross? How can you be willing to move beyond the norm to serve and converse with your in-law?

3. How might God want you to show flexibility in your relationship with your in-law?

4. What steps can you take this month to love your husband or son by loving your in-law?

5. When you think of your in-law, have you treated communication with her as a means to communion? If not, what has been your real goal when you communicate with her? What does this reveal about your broader view of communication with God?

6. Consider the eight ways to nurture communion with your in-law listed in this chapter. Which comes easiest to you? Which feels hardest? Why? How might you cultivate growth in your area of weakness?

CONFLICT

Making Peace like Christ

The year was 2020, and the world was reeling from a global pandemic. Holly could feel her heart skip a beat as the car pulled into their driveway. Her mother-in-law, Donna, was coming for an extended visit after a year without seeing each other. It wasn't that she didn't love Donna, but she often felt like she was being dissected under a microscope when they were together. Whether it was passive-aggressive comments about her less than organized house, "suggestions" on the kids' bedtime routine, or overt critiques about her cooking, Holly often felt judged and beaten up.

This visit held extra anticipation after a year without seeing each other. Donna wasn't nearly as cautious as Holly and felt like Holly's requests to keep the family quarantined had been extreme. Didn't she value seeing family more than being healthy? Would her grandkids still show her the same warmth and love after so many months apart?

Smiles spread on everyone's faces as Donna walked up to the porch step. "Grandma is here! Grandma is here!" the kids shouted with enthusiasm. Yet within moments, icy tension filled the air.

"Donna, we're so happy to see you! We've missed you! Would you mind using this hand sanitizer before hugging everyone?"

Donna was dumbfounded, "You mean to say that I'm not allowed to hug my own son? Or grandchildren?"

As Holly fumbled over her explanation the tension mounted. Holly's husband walked into the living room in the midst of the conflict. "Steve—your wife says that I can't hug you, or I'll contaminate you." Anger bubbled up inside of Holly as she watched her mother-in-law twist her words in front of the children. She felt disrespected in her own household, and to make matters worse, Steve didn't come to her defense.

How was she going to make it through a week-long visit after a start like this?

The Source of All Conflict

Whether it's Holly and Donna or our in-law and us, where does conflict really begin? Is it just the result of differing opinions or passions or gifts? The gospel of Matthew gives us a clue of the origin of our tiffs and grudges. Our words and the acts that follow stem from our hearts. Matthew 15:18–19 tells us, "But what comes out of the mouth proceeds from the heart, and this defiles a person. For out of the heart come evil thoughts, murder, adultery, sexual immorality, theft, false witness, slander" (ESV). It's a weighty and convicting truth. When our emotions are out of control and our mouth is running rampant, we have to look at the mirror of our own hearts. What thing have we wanted so badly, that we made it an idol in our life? An *idol* is defined as "any desire that has grown into a consuming demand that rules our hearts; it is something we think we must have to be happy, fulfilled, or secure."[1] Whether it's a vacation sans kids, money for a kitchen update, or a peaceful relationship with our in-laws, our good desires can easily become ultimate. Our sense of entitlement leads us to bitter disappointment when we're not treated the way we think we deserve. We tighten our grip on our idols for fear that something, or someone, will mess up our perfect plan.

James 4:1–2 further illuminates what causes conflict between us: "What is the source of wars and fights among you? Don't they come from your passions that wage war within you? You desire and do not have. You murder and covet and cannot obtain. You fight and wage war. You do not have because you do not ask." Our natural, fleshly tendency is to look out for ourselves. The pride in our hearts makes us aware of the sins of our in-law but fails to see our own part in the conflict. We have warring desires—whether it's spending Easter at your mother-in-law's house or your mom's house. And when we're not walking in step with the Spirit to address those desires, we default into selfish quarreling. Said another way, sin is in every human heart, waging war on the inside, and when left unchecked, it creates conflicts on the outside. As long as sin is in the world, conflicts will be. They should not surprise us. They are a part of life in a sin-stricken world. And so if there is no way around them in this life, the question becomes, then, how to rightly view them and how to biblically handle them.

Conflict—An Inevitable Opportunity

When two sinners are in a relationship together, conflict is inevitable. Even in the best of relationships there is bound to be disagreement, hurt feelings, and stepped-on toes. And, of so many types of relationships in this world, the in-law relationship is unique. We don't have a choice of who our mother-in-law will be or who our child will pick for a spouse. Often times we've dreamed up the ideal in-law in our mind, and the reality of our family member falls short of what we imagined. As we've discussed before, we might have different family backgrounds, educations, and dreams for the future. The merging of two families brings together different holiday traditions, ways of raising children, and methods of handling money. And with those differences comes all sorts of conflicts.

So when those conflicts come down the pike—and they will—how should we view them? Should we only look at conflict as an annoying problem? Or is there a better way to view it? A wise way to view conflict, according to biblical conflict expert Ken Sande (whose work we are indebted to throughout this entire chapter)[2] is as an *opportunity*. An opportunity for what, you may ask? For growth. Have you ever looked at conflict that way? As God creates each person in his image, he blesses them with unique gifts, personalities, and preferences. It's this very diversity that completes the body of Christ. We lean on each other and the different gifts we bring. We learn from each other's unique backgrounds and perspectives. We show preference to one another by having an amenable spirit and deferring to others. Disagreements allow our thinking to be sharpened and our ideas to be widened. If this is true for the body of Christ in general, then it is certainly true between in-laws. "The Bible teaches that we should see conflict neither as an inconvenience nor as an occasion to force our will on others, but rather as an opportunity to demonstrate the love and power of God in our lives,"[3] says Ken Sande.

What if we believed that? Can you imagine what might change in our relationships? When disagreements arise with our in-law, what if we saw it as an opportunity to extend the grace of God, choosing to show love even when we disagree?

What if we saw it as a chance to grow more into the image of Christ our Peacemaker, putting into the practice the way *he* makes peace? Think about it: to better emulate Christ our Peacemaker, we need opportunities to make peace with someone we are at odds with! How else are we going to learn to better reflect this facet of his character? It is through our conflicts that God matures us and transforms us to the image of Christ. We can trust that God is using our in-law conflicts as a way to test our faith, produce perseverance, and mature us to be the woman he created us to be (James 1:2–4).

But to make good on these opportunities to extend God's grace and emulate Christ our Peacemaker, we need to do a little thinking on how God himself makes peace.

How God Makes Peace with Us

God gives us the ultimate example of a peacemaker through his Son. We who were once his enemies, separated from God due to the sin in our hearts, were brought near by the blood of Christ. No matter how many good deeds we do, money we give away, or kind words we speak, no one except Christ can bridge the gap between sinners and a holy God. He is the ultimate peacemaker, the one who made a way when there was no way.

As Paul explains in Ephesians 2:12–19, the gospel brings peace vertically between us and God, as well as horizontally among those who are in conflict with each other. Take a look for yourself:

> At that time you were without Christ, excluded
> from the citizenship of Israel, and foreigners
> to the covenants of promise, without hope
> and without God in the world. But now in

Christ Jesus, you who were far away have been brought near by the blood of Christ. For he is our peace, who made both groups one and tore down the dividing wall of hostility. In his flesh, he made of no effect the law consisting of commands and expressed in regulations, so that he might create in himself one new man from the two, resulting in peace. He did this so that he might reconcile both to God in one body through the cross by which he put the hostility to death. He came and proclaimed the good news of peace to you who were far away and peace to those who were near. For through him we both have access in one Spirit to the Father. So, then, you are no longer foreigners and strangers, but fellow citizens with the saints, and members of God's household.

In verses 12 and 13, Paul makes it clear that one party—the Gentiles—are made right with God through Christ. They were once far away from him, but now they are brought near. Yet that's not all. In verses 14–19, Paul goes on to say that this Gentile group is now made right with another group they were once at odds with—the Jews. Jesus did not only reconcile them with God, but with their enemies, too! He has "broken down the dividing wall of hostility" between the two parties, making them "both one" through his sacrifice.

Just as the divisions between Jews and Gentiles were erased through the blood of Christ, the cross of Christ reconciles us to those who seem completely different than ourselves, including our in-law! It brings peace to tense relationships, rest where there has been strife. And did you notice *how* this peace is made? Jesus makes peace not through retaliation or withdrawal, but through sacrifice. He sets the pattern for our posture in conflict—one that should always be sacrificial and restorative. We look for ways to lay down our rights in order to bridge the gap with the other person. We take the apostle Paul's advice in Philippians 2:3–4, that we "do nothing from selfish ambition or conceit, but in humility count others more significant than yourselves. Let each of you look not only to his own interests, but also to the interests of others" (ESV).

If we're going to do peacemaking God's way (whether with our in-law or anyone else), instead of demanding our rights, we follow Christ's example by yielding our rights. We look to serve our in-law instead of rake them over the coals. Our goal isn't to win the argument or get what we want, but to restore peace in the relationship.

As Christians, if we know this is God's way of peacemaking, why is it so hard for us to follow it? Let's begin our answer to that by starting with a wedding story.

The Wedding of Whose Dreams?

Kelsey and Tim fell wildly in love their senior year of college. They got engaged shortly after graduation, but had to wait over a year for their wedding due to internships in different states. As they video-chatted throughout the year, the excitement of wedding planning helped their time apart go faster. Kelsey loved the idea of an outdoor wedding on a riverboat. But the fall was the first time available, and the state was Minnesota. They knew it was risky, but still planned their riverboat fall wedding, hoping the weather would cooperate. As they shared their exciting plans with Tim's mom, Joyce, awkward silence filled the air.

"A riverboat wedding in the fall?" she asked. "What if it's too cold to be outside? All of your guests will freeze! I was thinking our church would work well."

Kelsey and Tim politely listened to Joyce's perspective, but insisted they had thought things through and were willing to take a risk. As the wedding drew near, Joyce looked for ways she could be involved. She couldn't help but feel left out as Kelsey's mom spearheaded the decorations and menu planning.

When the wedding day finally arrived, it was hovering at 50 degrees with a chance of rain. Joyce kept thinking to herself, *Why didn't they listen to my advice? The wedding will be ruined by this awful weather!*

Kelsey and Tim were so delighted to be getting married, the less-than-ideal weather didn't matter to them. They could sense Joyce's displeasure over the forecast and an "I told-you-so" attitude. But they tried to give grace and move forward without complaining.

When the drizzle began, Joyce's annoyance turned to resentment. How could her daughter-in-law have been so selfish to plan her dream wedding, without thinking about the comfort of her guests? As the day went on, Joyce found other things to add to her list of wrongs—her family wasn't seated next to the head table like Kelsey's was, the menu didn't accommodate her gluten-free preference, and the newly married couple chose not to go to each table at the reception to greet their guests.

As Joyce's resentment grew, Kelsey could sense it, and she devolved into further withdrawal, putting more distance between herself and Joyce. She leaned only into the help of those she hand-picked, and sometimes even turned a blind eye to the needs of her guests in order to avoid discomfort.

Unfortunately, Kelsey and Tim's wedding day turned into the beginning of years of conflict in their relationship with Joyce.

The World's Way of Handling Relational Wars

Both Kelsey and Joyce are believers, yet when it comes to how they handled their conflict, they didn't choose the pattern of Christ our Peacemaker—the way of sacrifice. If we're honest, we're all a lot like them, aren't we? We know that Jesus resolved our conflict with God through sacrifice. We know that's the right way. Yet choosing this way is hard, because the world gives us a multitude of unhelpful ways of dealing with conflict, many of which we learned growing up—avoidance, escapism, denial, aggressive outbursts, or passive-aggressiveness. I confess in my (Stacy) relationship with my MIL, sometimes it seems easier to ignore the issue than deal with it. It can be easy to pretend like a problem doesn't exist, all the while letting tension build between the two of us.

When conflict occurs, most of us trend to one side or the other. We either verbally explode (*aggressive outbursts*) or sweep things under the rug (*avoidance, escapism*).[4] Instead of resolving conflict the way Christ does, our sinful nature bends toward one of these worldly extremes. And at times we bend differently, depending on who the relationship is with. Our spouse might be the recipient of aggressive outbursts while we use passive-aggressive tactics with our in-law. Some of us dislike conflict so much that we try to pretend it doesn't exist. We might avoid talking about a delicate issue, end the relationship, or find other ways to run away from the problem. Instead of peace-making, we're "peace-faking," as Ken Sande likes to put it.[5]

I (Stacy) know I've done this before. Instead of hashing out a conflict with Barb, I can let resentment build because I don't want to use the short time we have together on things I perceive as negative. I forget that conflict isn't all negative; it's a good opportunity to become more like Jesus and extend God's grace. And so I let the conflict go unaddressed. Yet it is still there, all the same. The same is true for the example of Kelsey and Joyce—they let resentment grow in the dark, poisoning the relationship, instead of handling the issue in the light and reconciling. They didn't use the opportunity they had to make peace according to the way of their Savior. Can you imagine how different the day—and the years following—would have been if Kelsey and Joyce were more focused on sacrificing for the other instead of keeping their defenses up?

The opposite of escaping from conflict is aggression. Those of us who tend toward this extreme are "in it to win it." We want to get our point across, no matter what the consequences entail. This might be shown through explosive words, *gossip* and *slander*, or in extreme cases, even physical assault. Aggressive tactics can feel like being plowed over by the more dominant person. A less volatile but equally damaging method is passive aggressiveness. Dropping hints about disagreements, trying to manipulate a situation through words or giving someone the cold shoulder can all be methods of trying to win via passive hostility.

Think back to our opening illustration. Holly's request for Donna to use hand sanitizer resulted in an angry explosion of words. Donna's accusations that she couldn't even hug her own son were meant to shame Holly for having a more cautious standard than herself. And sadly, Donna shamed Holly in front of her own children. How much hurt could have been avoided if Donna had deferred to Holly's request, or if Holly let go of some of her cleanliness standards for the sake of family unity—or perhaps chatted with Donna beforehand, explaining her fears in an open way, giving Donna a heads-up for what to expect when walking through the front door, and asking for her grace in a season of personal uneasiness? Or even after the moment of conflict, how could the whole visit have changed for the better if the two women pulled away for a moment and simply discussed the issue directly, between the two of them, in gentleness and respect?

The world's methods of handling conflict will only cause more strife and heartache. Just like the temptation of sin, they promise happiness but ultimately leave us miserable. Thankfully the Bible doesn't leave us without a roadmap of how to handle conflict. To get practical, let's consider the path God provides to encourage peace-making in our relationships.

Practical Steps for Making Peace with Your In-Law[6]

1. Remove the Log (Matt. 7:5)

Our sinful nature makes it easy to see what the other person has done wrong while neglecting to see our part in the conflict. We criticize and judge, self-righteously condemning our opponents and fail to examine our own heart. It's hard to admit our wrong, but that's exactly what Jesus says we need to do when involved in a conflict.

> "Why do you look at the splinter in your brother's eye but don't notice the beam of wood in your own eye? Or how can you say to your brother, 'Let me take the splinter out of your eye,' and look, there's a beam of wood in your own eye! Hypocrite! First take the beam of wood out of your eye, and then you will see

clearly to take the splinter out of your brother's eye." (Matt. 7:3–5)

The first step in making peace with our in-law is looking in the mirror. Ask God to show you your own sin (Ps. 139:23–24). Or ask a trusted friend to help you see where you may be at fault in the conflict. Sometimes we need a fresh set of eyes or someone not personally involved to make an honest assessment. Ask yourself the hard questions . . .

> *Why am I so angry about this?*
> *What kind of behavior am I relying on to get what I want?*
> *How am I trying to rationalize my wrongs?*
> *Where am I shifting blame?*
> *What am I hoping to gain?*
> *What war is going on inside of me?*
> *How could I have responded differently?*

Humbly admit where you've been wrong and turn away from your sin. Conflict is a two-way street. First John 1:8 reminds us that if we claim to be without sin, we are only deceiving ourselves and we're not really Christians! That's a weighty warning when we're tempted to overlook our own role in conflict.

2. Overlook Her Offense If Possible (Prov. 19:11)

Maybe you've been hurt by your in-law. How do you decide whether to talk about it or let it go? At times, we follow the instruction of Proverbs 19:11—to overlook the offense. When there is a minor offense, a misunderstanding, or personality differences, we can move forward by not dwelling on our hurt.

We extend grace to our in-law just as God extends grace to us—forgiving, moving on, and not bringing up the offense again. We remember the unconditional love Jesus has for us that enables us to forgive others.

While we were still his enemies, Jesus poured out his love and mercy on us through his death on the cross. He forgave our most heinous sins. He is rich in mercy, slow to anger, abounding in lovingkindness. One way we can grow in Christlikeness is to emulate this forgiveness. The Bible is filled with exhortations to overlook an offense . . .

> "A person's insight gives him patience, and his virtue is to overlook an offense" (Prov. 19:11).

> "A fool's displeasure is known at once, but whoever ignores an insult is sensible" (Prov. 12:16).

> "A hot-tempered person stirs up conflict, but one slow to anger calms strife" (Prov. 15:18).

> "To start a conflict is to release a flood; stop the dispute before it breaks out" (Prov. 17:14).

> "Hatred stirs up conflict, but love covers all offenses" (Prov. 10:12).

> "Above all, maintain constant love for one another, since love covers a multitude of sins" (1 Pet. 4:8).

Ask God to help you treat your in-law with the same love and kindness that you would like to be treated with. Confess your own pride that can be so easily wounded and look to serve and love your in-law as if nothing happened.

But what if the offense seems too big to overlook? How do we know what to overlook and what to gently confront? We can pray and ask the Lord for discernment. He promises to give us wisdom when we ask (James 1:5). Generally speaking, when the offense is an isolated instance, and relatively minor, ask the Lord for grace to be merciful, just as he is merciful to you (Matt. 5:7). We have all done things to wound each other. Wouldn't you want someone to extend grace to you for an unintentional wound?

However, if you are consistently hurt through a pattern of comments or actions by your in-law, it's likely time to bring the issue up. Don't allow seeds of bitterness to take root in your heart. If a wall seems to be growing between the two of you, and you find yourself harboring resentment or avoiding interactions, it's time to gently talk the issue through.

3. Go to Her Directly (Matt. 18:15)

When we're upset with our in-law, our natural tendency can be to go tell someone else about it, to get it off our chest. Maybe as an authentic prayer request, or maybe as a form of gossip or slander. But the biblical model is to first go to God with our sin, confessing our own wrongdoing and asking for his help as we talk to the other person. Then Jesus directs us to go directly to the person who sinned against us for a one-on-one conversation: "If your brother sins against you, go tell him his fault, between you and him alone" (Matt. 18:15). The hope is for restoration in the relationship.

Most of the time these kinds of meetings are best done face-to-face. So much can be miscommunicated through emails and text messages. You can't hear the tone of the other person. Words come across differently in print rather than in person. Communication will be most effective when we can look the other person in the eye and express love and gentleness with our demeanor. It may be tempting to go everywhere but her, but friend, believe your Bible. After you've gone to God, go to your in-law.

4. Restore Gently (Gal. 6:1)

Our culture prides itself on its own version of speaking "truth"—making snarky and pointed remarks meant to demean others via tweets or other social media platforms. Words are often used for tearing down instead of building up. It's easy to bring that combativeness into difficult situations we find ourselves in, including in-law conflict.

Instead of marching into our meeting with a list of grievances, the biblical way is to enter the meeting with a humble heart, willing to both listen and offer loving admonitions for our in-law. And we do this with a gentle spirit: "Brothers and sisters, if someone is overtaken in any wrongdoing, you who are spiritual, restore such a person with a gentle spirit" (Gal. 6:1). To be gentle is to be kind, tender, gracious, calm, and not harsh or combative.[7] Proverbs 15:1 tells us that a gentle answer turns away anger. "Pleasant words are a honeycomb, sweet to the taste and health to the body" (Prov. 16:24). A gentle tone can diffuse an otherwise explosive situation. It makes the conversation healing and restorative instead of a battle to be won. Owning up to our own wrongdoing while softly correcting our in-law will go a long way in building a bridge.

And notice that the goal of all this gentleness—it is not to berate or condemn or shame or put someone in their place, but to "restore." If your in-law has been stuck in a pattern of sinning against you, consider this: being caught in sin strains their relationship with God. They are missing out on the fullness of what they could be experiencing with him, and part of correcting them in a gentle way is to restore them back to not only a peaceful relationship with you, but with God too. Is your goal in conflict resolution the other person's *restoration*? If not, it's not biblical conflict resolution. Helping your in-law see her sin isn't really about you, though it certainly affects you. It's ultimately about her well-being with God. Restore her gently, as you'd want someone to restore you.

5. Forgive Fully

True forgiveness means letting go of the hurt done to you. It means not dwelling on it, not mentioning it, not looking to repay evil with evil but choosing to give grace instead. It's trusting that God is our avenger (Rom. 12:19), so we don't need to pay back the one who hurt us.

God sets a high bar for forgiveness, calling us to forgive just as he has forgiven us (Eph. 4:32). When we were still his enemies, he died for us (Rom. 5:8)! As far as the east is from the west, so far has he removed our sins from us (Ps. 103:12).

We cannot forgive based on our own willpower. Time and time again we'll resort to dwelling on the wrongs done to us and harboring bitterness toward our offender. But by the supernatural grace of God, we can choose forgiveness. We can ask God to give us the ability to love our in-law despite how we've been treated. And in doing so, we show the depth of our own relationship with God. "Our gratitude for what God gives us is revealed in how merciful we are toward those who owe us. Our horizontal relationship with one another reveals the nature of our vertical one with God."[8]

The pardon we've received from God should spur us on to freely forgive those who have wounded us. When we fully forgive our in-law, we relinquish our right to get even, to give them the cold shoulder, or to hold their sin over their head. Instead we move toward them in love, treating them as we would want to be treated, covering over the offense with love. The scoreboard is erased and we are freed from the prison of bitterness.

Can you imagine all that could have looked different in the lives of Holly, Donna, Kelsey, and Joyce if they had made peace in a biblical way? Can you imagine what might look different in your life if you approached every conflict with your in-law as an opportunity to put Christ our Peacemaker on display? It may be hard. It may be other-worldly. But resolving conflict God's way is worth it. And it bears fruit! ✎

Discussion Questions

1. When you think of the "wars and fights" happening in your life—whether with your in-law or anyone else—what would you say the source of these conflicts is? What's causing them? How does your answer square with James 4:1?

2. Why do you think it's easy to blame others as the source of our conflicts?

3. How do you typically view conflicts in general? How has this chapter influenced the way you view them moving forward?

4. Re-read Ephesians 2:12–18. Those who were far away are "brought near" by what? What does blood signify?

5. If Christ's death-to-self and sacrifice is what created relational closeness between us and God, what does that imply for the relational closeness we want to experience with our in-law who might feel "far off" right now?

6. Recall the worldly ways of handling relational conflict. Which side of the spectrum do you tend toward? Why?

7. Which of the five practical steps for peacemaking is hardest for you? Why? Which of these steps do you need to implement with your in-law this week or month?

A NEW GENERATION

How a Mother-in-Law Can Come Alongside Her Daughter-in-Law

My (Barb) first pregnancy went smoothly. I thought I was sailing through my second pregnancy too, until the last trimester, when a routine ultrasound revealed a serious concern. My doctor ordered bed rest. How would our rambunctious two-year-old son survive with Mommy in bed for three months? My husband had always pitched in around the house. But how could he work his long hours and manage all the household chores? We needed help!

That's when my mother-in-law Rose arrived. Even after six years of my marriage to her son, I'm sure Rose wondered as much as I did, "When will our relationship reach a place of understanding?" Despite her fragile health, over the next two weeks, Rose kept up with my active toddler. She read him countless stories; they went for walks. She cleaned. She cooked. She did the laundry. And on top of all that, she made time to talk to her frightened, emotional daughter-in-law.

Strangely, I can't remember any particular conversation. What I remember is that she shared her life with me. I listened to her spiritual lessons. I knew God was not far off. He could handle my high-risk pregnancy. I felt God's love in a new way.

I began to recognize something else—Rose loved me too. How did I know? When I needed her, she came. She served me and my family tirelessly. Now I can see, God wisely gave me this hard situation. He taught me about love. He graciously allowed my mother-in-law to show her love to me in a way that I could accept. He was showing me, preparing me, even, for what it might look like to come alongside a daughter-in-law.

New Roles and Relationship

In this chapter, we will seek to consider how God might use a mother-in-law in the life of her daughter-in-law. But before we start dreaming up what that might look like, let's consider some realities first.

The first reality is that as you walk this path with your DIL, the landscape under your feet is changing when it comes to your son. The ground will feel like it is rising and falling, and sometimes, tripping you up. And that's normal. See, relationships between mothers and daughters do not usually change much when daughters marry. Sure, they must make adjustments, but most still have a direct connection. Mother-son relationships are different. Their relationship almost always changes when the son marries. Moms must let go completely. Mothers are no longer first-string players; they are the support team. They are used to walking on the path of "primary," but now, all of a sudden, the path lowers to "secondary," and that path feels foreign.

At the same time the mother is adjusting to her "demotion," someone else is adjusting to a huge "promotion." The newlywed daughter-in-law now feels the path rising and shifting, moving her into new territory as "primary" in your son's life. That can feel disorienting for her too. To steady herself, she naturally leans on her close friends and family for support. She doesn't intend to slight her mother-in-law. But her MIL is likely the last person she would reach out to during such a transition for a number of reasons. Perhaps she wants to impress her MIL and does not want to communicate weakness. Perhaps she has a painful history with mother figures. Perhaps she is simply consumed with the early stages of creating a home, thinking about kids, pleasing her husband, and fitting in whatever job she may have.

As these paths change and new roles take shape, insecurities and disorientation are experienced on both sides as each woman tries to get her footing, and that's okay. But is there hope? Can these two women lean on God to make this relationship work? Yes and yes.

The Reality of Difference

Along with new roles, there's another reality at play for a mother-in-law to consider: differences. Most women come into the in-law relationship barely knowing each other. Like all strangers, getting to know each other takes time. Different personalities, life experiences, and viewpoints may delay the process even more. A young wife longs to start her own Christmas traditions while a mother-in-law insists on the yearly Christmas Eve gathering. A mother-in-law wants to lovingly bake a birthday cake for her son while his young wife splurges on a bakery cake she thinks tastes better. A young wife prefers texting. The mother-in-law values talking. What happens when the things one generation views as essential, the other doesn't even like?

We see life differently in each new decade. You may have worried that menopause would leave your brain foggy and are surprised that your mind is clearer now than ever before. You feel like your years have taught you something. On the flip side, your DIL sees life from her moment in time, and that's not a deficiency on her part. It's right where God wants her. She sees life through a certain lens, and her years on this earth have taught her things too.

When I look back on my own relationship with my parents during those early years as a wife and mom, I wish both sides would have made room for differences, celebrating them instead of feeling threatened by them. I was a child of the fifties and sixties and a young woman of the seventies. What my parents' generation considered crazy is normal today. Natural childbirth, breastfeeding, working, and ministering outside the home, all took courage for me. I cringed when my parents complained, "How long do you plan to shelter your children? Why are you afraid to let them grow up in the normal way?" Sometimes, it seemed, the differences between our generations was only room for hurtful fodder. Yet I was guilty of the same mentality sometimes. Looking back, I see that Ron and I could have benefited from their experience in a myriad of circumstances. But to be honest I'm not sure that we asked, simply because we, too, considered the differences between us a threat instead of a gift.

The truth is, God gives both mother-in-law and daughter-in-law qualities that can help the other, if they'd only value one another's differences. If your heart is to come alongside your DIL in this season, take heart. Your job is not to minimize her differences so that she gets closer and closer to your mold. Nor is it to ignore her differences altogether, as if the act of noticing them is a mistake. Your aim is to notice them—face the reality that they are there—and then use them for good! What differences do you see in your DIL? How can you use those differences to move toward her instead of away?

The Reality of Technology

In the last section we talked about the reality of differences between MIL and DIL. Those are due to a variety of factors—age matters of course, but so does personality, giftedness, background, ethnicity, and culture. And we've learned that whatever our general differences, we can attempt to help and love one another.[1]

But there's one specific difference between MIL and DIL, especially in this particular moment in time, that warrants room for further discussion. And that is the reality of technology. The digital age marks a huge divide in our culture. Young women today were born into a rapidly changing world. Most prize doing things their way. They're used to customizing everything. When you grow up being told you can do and be anything, the burdens of adulthood come as a rude shock. But goals for school, career, community involvement, and marriage make unexpected demands on them. The schedule for their children is as crazy busy as their own. The family has little down time.

Women born before smartphones see the world differently. As latchkey kids, many learned to care for themselves at an early age. They grew up before the time when losing teams get a trophy, so they do not always expect praise. The demands of the family's monthly budget make job security important. Most look for ways to improve and want to keep growing. They learned the importance of interpersonal skills. After all, the guys who started Google and Facebook were still in school.[2]

Sally reflected, "As young wives, we asked friends, parents, and grandparents for advice." Google and Pinterest, friends and doctors are her daughter-in-law's go-to advisers. With a hint of remorse, Sally observes, "Social media tells her what to value and what to buy. And guess what, nine times out of ten, that advice is better than what I could offer." She goes on, "It's not just that I miss the pleasure of being asked for advice. It's the joy of passing on a little bit of who I am—as a child of God—to the next generation." If you are a mother-in-law in Sally's situation, what can you do?

I have felt this way too. And I've found that the situation is not hopeless. I've found that we can work in two directions: meeting our DIL on her digital turf (where you might find something new!) and also inviting her to our interpersonal turf (where she might enjoy a break from screens!). What could this look like? It could look like commenting on her social media post as she seeks advice about a recipe or an item she might buy. If that's where she's throwing out a question, be a seasoned voice that weighs in. Show up in her digital space sometimes. Other times, invite her into screenless situations that feel more comfortable to you. Ask her to help you bake an old family recipe or take a walk around the park. Those are the kinds of places lifelong wisdom comes out naturally.

Or consider another situation between Stacy and myself. Stacy began doing virtual Bible studies online, and at first, I resisted. I wondered, "Why change a reliable method of Bible study?" God's Word is the foundation to all we know and do as believers. God has revealed himself to us in it. We can never adequately plumb its depths. But formal instruction—the kind where the teacher is right in front of you and you gather in-person with a group—is not the only way to teach biblical truth. When I gave Stacy's online Bible study a chance, I was encouraged to see the way God's Word was spreading to others (especially during the COVID-19 pandemic, when people couldn't gather in person). While nothing can replace in-person relationships with other believers, it is amazing to see the next generation sharing the Word of God in their digital spaces. Now, when Stacy leads a virtual Bible study, I'm there. (She also unfailingly comes to my rescue when I have social media questions!)

The Reality of Your Own Limited Perspective

Take it from me, by the time a woman is fifty, she's made enough mistakes that she has a wealth of knowledge to share. There's nothing wrong with wanting to pass down your wisdom as a MIL. But no one knows everything. As you consider how to come alongside your DIL, remember that your perspective is limited, just like everybody else's. No matter how much a mother-in-law knows, her daughter-in-law can teach her a lot. For me, that looks like learning new recipes from Stacy and learning from her knowledge of the Word. For you, it may look different, depending on the strengths of your DIL. The goal is being willing to receive, not only give.

Remember: God doesn't just have help and perspective waiting for *her* in this relationship. He has those things for you too! He is equally committed to helping you along as you come alongside her. Don't lock yourself out of that. God has put her in your life!

If you ask God, he will show you how you can grow in love and respect for your DIL, being willing to receive sometimes instead of just giving. He has given each of you different gifts, not to benefit you, but to benefit others. God expects us to use our gifts for the good of others (1 Cor. 12:12–27). How often do you acknowledge and celebrate what God is doing through your in-law? As you look to God, he will enable you to appreciate your in-law's gifts, "with no sense of envy, rivalry, superiority or inferiority, because this is the kind of love sharing among Father, Son, and Spirit."[3]

What if the barriers persist? Ultimately the battle is not with your in-law. The battle is in your heart. Identify your problem. Is it self-pity? Is it self-centeredness? Fear in admitting you are limited in perspective? Whatever afflicts you, let God fill you with his love. Ask God to soften your heart. He will enable you to listen, observe, and learn from your in-law. The Holy Spirit alone can bring the change that you need.

Now that we've considered some realities at play in the relationship—new roles, general differences, and technological differences—let's consider the power a MIL wields when it comes to words, forgiveness, encouragement, and service in the life of her DIL.

Love in So Many Words

At one time your children listened to your words of wisdom. Maybe you imagined being the go-to sage for the family. Now, it sometimes seems that your adult son doesn't listen to you at all. Nobody wants your hard-learned advice! You are a mother-in-law—that dreaded word! Every time you open your mouth, things get worse. Stop and think: have you considered the power of your words? How are you using that power right now? To dismiss or belittle your daughter-in-law? Even a wise spiritual lesson when spoken condescendingly tears down respect. You both lose. In-law relationships are fragile. No matter how strong you think your in-law is, she requires loving care and loving words.

Consider Amy and her daughter-in-law, Rebekah. Amy knew what it was like to have anxiety dominate your life. She empathized with the battle her daughter-in-law, Rebekah, was fighting and wanted to help. Amy had learned to depend on God in new ways and wanted Rebekah to know the same freedom of trusting God. Amy sent her favorite Scripture verses to Rebekah. At family gatherings, she brought up the topic of anxiety often and consistently advised Rebekah how to handle her weakness. Amy was sure she knew just what Rebekah needed. So why did her words come out all wrong? Perhaps it's because Amy never stopped to consider the timing, the tone, or the frequency of her well-meant words. Perhaps it's also because in all her talking, Amy never stopped to listen to Rebekah. Words that Amy thought were instructive came across as condescension. Rebekah felt condemned in her weakness. She felt policed and monitored by Amy, not lovingly understood. Now whenever Amy texted, Rebekah hit "delete."

Spoken without insight and at the wrong time, well-meant words can cause harm. We can all take to heart Proverbs 14:1: "Every wise woman builds her house, but a foolish one tears it down with her own hands." Do you want to be the wise woman who builds? Observe your words. Jesus says our words reveal the truth about our heart (Matt. 12:34). If we're smart, we will believe him. As we consider our words to our DIL, we'll ponder what they reveal about our hearts, and no matter what we find there, we won't turn away from what Jesus shows us about ourselves. We'll do the work of repentance, and fight to keep our heart right. And as we do this, we'll become more like Jesus in our speech to our DIL (and anyone else!), which is the whole point. Our loving heavenly Father wants to use this process of considering your words and your heart to make you someone who loves like Jesus loves.

Learning to love like Jesus is never comfortable. Consider Rena. Her daughter-in-law grew up in a home where hurtful words were common. The thoughtless words she spoke to

Rena proved it. When her DIL rejected her or used her words in unkind ways, Rena often cried. Her DIL always apologized a few days later, but the sting in their relationship lingered. Rena's friends said she needed to confront her DIL or she'd never change. Rena was torn. Didn't love mean God expected her to ignore her DIL's outburst? Gradually, Rena learned that love sometimes remains silent and other times it speaks the truth (Eph. 4:15). She also learned to look at Jesus. After all, our Savior was ignored, mistreated, and disrespected by the words of others too. What did he do? He kept loving.

For Rena and every mother-in-law, it helps to remember that loving as Jesus loved means we do not insist on our own way (1 Cor. 13:5). Like Jesus, we do not seek our own advantage, but that of others, that they may be saved (1 Cor. 10:33). We repent of resentment. We pray for power to forgive our in-law as freely as God forgives us. In Christ, God does not count our many, many sins against us (2 Cor. 5:19). Through the years of looking to Jesus and following his lead on what each situation requires, God has drawn both Rena and her DIL closer to himself and each other. And the same is possible for you and for me.

Both Amy and Rena are learning different lessons when it comes to the power of words. One is learning how to go slower, sharing words of wisdom at the right time and in the right tone. The other is learning how to speak up, lovingly addressing the issue of unhealthy communication in a way that is healthy, all while looking to Christ as her guide. And in both cases, we see just how mightily God works through words (and the heart behind them!).

Forgive

God allows us all to go through tense times. Child-rearing, daily scheduling, money management, church, health issues, community involvement—any change can create a crisis. How will we react? Most times, we feel the pull to respond in entitlement or retaliation. Whatever the situation, we feel like the focus of the solution should revolve around us—our needs, our pain, our struggles, our schedules. And when we don't see our DIL considering these things, we feel hurt. So we retaliate somehow. Maybe by stewing on things, giving the silent treatment, withdrawing emotionally, being passive-aggressive, buddying up with the other favored DIL and subtly rubbing her nose in it, lashing out in sarcasm (or even fits of rage), or gossiping with friends.

Yet the call of Christ is for us to turn away from all those worldly ways of handling things and instead, forgive freely. Forgive freely? How can we do what is impossible? The gospel tells us that Jesus has done the impossible for us (Rom. 4:8). The cross demonstrates God's love to us (Rom. 5:8). As a human being, Jesus overcame evil with good by the power of the Holy Spirit (Rom. 12:21). God expects us to follow his example. By his grace, with his Spirit, you *can* forgive. What if emotions tempt you to say words you will regret? What if fear says your in-law will never change? Ask God for faith to take hope. Ask God for your life more and more to include love, joy, peace, patience, kindness, goodness, faithfulness, gentleness, and self-control (Gal. 5:22–23). As you depend on God, he will change your thoughts and give you joy in obedience (2 Cor. 10:5).

One of the best things you can model in front of your DIL is obedience to Christ and forgiveness toward others, even when it hurts. Even when she's the source of the hurt. You never know—perhaps she never had this kind of example before now. Maybe the way you consistently shower her in undeserved forgiveness will be the thing that draws her closer to Christ!

Encourage

Remember Sally? She argued, "I know I'm to keep on loving her as Jesus has loved me. But I can't help feeling sorry for myself. It seems like I'm unwanted. It's not that I want to be the 'expert in residence.' All I want is for her to show interest. I don't know where I fit in. I can't help but feel like I've been demoted."

Moses was God's man. At great cost to himself, he had led God's people for forty years. Yet it was time for a new leader. God had chosen Joshua to succeed him. When Moses announced his replacement to God's people, he did so with grace and trust. He never resented Joshua. Even before Joshua actually replaced him, Moses had worked hard to help and build up Joshua. Moses made sure the people respected Joshua. He did not allow himself to feel set aside. No matter what, it was God's time for the new generation and Moses's role needed to change.

> Moses then summoned Joshua and said to him in the sight of all Israel, "Be strong and courageous, for you will go with this people into the land the LORD swore to give to their ancestors. You will enable them to take possession of it. The LORD is the one who will go before you. He will be with you; he will not leave you or abandon you. Do not be afraid or discouraged." (Deut. 31:7–8)

Moses's words are full of concern for Joshua with no thought for himself. Moses embraced the change. His identity was not wrapped up in his leadership but in knowing he belonged to God. Your role change does not mean you have no more value or purpose. Change is never all loss. Anticipate your new role with a sense of relief. Consider this: God is lightening your burden. You are free to enjoy the love of others without the weight of full responsibility. Remember Moses. God has given you the responsibility to encourage your son and daughter-in-law to be strong and courageous.

What is encouragement? To encourage means to "inspire courage." Moses told Joshua to have courage and not be afraid. God would never leave him or let him go. As a mother-in-law, you could run down the list of what you've lost: status, control, and influence. You could complain that your family doesn't value you anymore. You may wonder: "What is my calling now?" Your role has changed, but God's good plan for you and your family has not. Never fear—your family needs your contribution. You may see only loss but consider your new privileges. God has freed you to cultivate a relationship with your daughter-in-law and encourage her relationship with your son. And as hard as they try to put on a good face and pull it all together in these younger years of chaos, *they need that encouragement*. You needed it back then. Joshua needed it as he entered into a new season of taking the mantle. We all need it in times of transition.

The world and the devil will relentlessly try to evoke fear, confusion, and despair in their lives—be the voice that inspires courage. Often. They need it so much more than they even realize.

Serve

Years ago, I (Barb) wanted to finish my nursing degree from home. I was focused and willing to put in extra hours, but we had three small children! As the time approached for my hospital practicum, the pressure grew intense. How would I manage hours at the hospital and care for my family? Asking for help was difficult. Enter Betty. My mother's age, Betty occasionally helped my friend with her small children. After I explained my need, Betty said she'd pray. The very next day she agreed to help, and said, "I'm simply following the Holy Spirit's leading." When Betty was with us, all was well.

Betty was different. She didn't pretend not to have problems. But she showed me what an incredible difference God's Word had made in her life. Her transparent communication meant I could approach her. Her faith was more than a correct belief system. I saw a woman on a personal journey with God. Watching Betty made me hungry to experience the living God. She did not read the Bible as a textbook, but to know and connect with God. She cared for her husband and her elderly mother but still invested so much time in me. Her service to our family left an indelible mark.

During the weeks of my practicum, Betty came to our home early every morning. With her guidance, chaotic school preparations became orderly. The kids felt secure. She knew when to be firm and when to flex. Betty lived out before me everything she had told me about Jesus. She put aside her personal comfort to follow Christ into this low-profile, unglamorous assignment. When I came home from the hospital, I'd find the children playing happily and dinner in the oven. I wondered why the floor never needed sweeping. Was Betty cleaning too?

No amount of money could have paid Betty for her service. We pulled together more than our meager budget could afford. On her last day, I handed her a check. Without even looking at the amount, she took the check and ripped it in half. My eyes filled with tears. Betty said she served us freely because of Jesus's service to her. Because Jesus loved her, she wanted her words and actions to show his love to us. She served us so that we might trust, obey, and enjoy Jesus.[4]

At best, most people see the in-law relationship as give and take. After all, we think, *No one served me.* By the time women become mothers-in-law, many are taking care of older family members. They are so ready to claim "me time."

Yet Scripture doesn't add exceptions to the call to serve others depending on one's phase of life. We are called to serve for as many days as we are Christians on this earth! So the question for us becomes, then, "How can I surrender my own interests to walk alongside my daughter-in law?" (Oh, and expect pushback from friends when you actually start living this out!) A mother-in-law's service to her daughter-in-law gives weight to her words. But serving the younger generation is not simply a way for them to love you.

Jesus reclined at the table ready to celebrate the Passover meal with his twelve disciples. He passed the bread and wine. Jesus "got up from supper, laid aside his outer clothing, took a towel, and tied it around himself. Next, he poured water into a basin and began to wash his disciples' feet and to dry them with the towel tied around him" (John 13:4–5). Why was Jesus washing feet? Wasn't this the job of a servant?

Jesus had told his disciples, "For even the Son of Man did not come to be served, but to serve, and to give his life as a ransom for many" (Mark 10:45). Now he said, "So if I, your Lord and Teacher, have washed your feet, you also ought to wash one another's feet. For I have given you an example, that you also should do just as I have done for you. . . . If you know these things, you are blessed if you do them" (John 13:14–15, 17). That night, through his own example, Jesus taught his disciples how they were to serve others.

God gives every mother-in-law an opportunity to become the servant in the room. We can show our daughter-in-law that we value her above ourselves. Scripture tell us, "Adopt the same attitude as that of Christ Jesus" (Phil. 2:5). We may think, *She should respect my ways (and wash my feet)! What if I don't have any energy left?* Or, *What if she takes advantage of me?* Jesus promised to bless those who serve others as he did. Can it be true? Jesus blesses us with his presence and care as we serve others. The servant's life is blessed by the presence and care of Jesus. Through us he produces eternal fruit (Ps. 1:3).[5]

What if your daughter-in-law fails to be grateful for your service? How easily we start to think, *If you aren't being the in-law you should be, don't complain if I am not being the in-law I should be.* Dare we admit it? We may not always feel love for our daughter-in-law. Consider this—the feeling of love many times follows the act of loving. Christ's love for his disciples when they all abandoned him. Think about his steady love for you over the years even when you've ignored him. To serve is an act of love that gains entry into a person's heart. And even if the worst happens— even if you're never appreciated in the end, you'll know you were faithful to your God and his Word. You'll know that you were a Betty—a person who carried the Spirit of God wherever she went, and that you at least modeled what staying the course looks like later in life instead of throwing in the towel.

From the Other Side: A Daughter-in-Law's Perspective

Having a mother-in-law who truly comes alongside me (Stacy) is a gift. I've learned so much from Barb and am grateful for the godly example she sets for our family. Barb has given mothers-in-law some great advice in this chapter. I'd also like to share what's been meaningful from my perspective.

There's never been a doubt in my mind that Barb is for me and not against me. She respects our marriage and doesn't compete with me for the attention of Ben (my husband). I'm more than grateful for a mother-in-law who diligently studies the Scripture and applies it to her life. Because I see the depth of Barb's relationship with God, I'm more eager to ask her advice in certain areas. We've sought her counsel on difficult parenting issues and ministry conflicts. She's careful not to offer opinions that are not sought out but has waited for us to ask. This helps increase my trust in her. Her simple words of encouragement in my role as wife and mom mean more than she knows.

One of the greatest gifts in our marriage has been her willingness to come and stay with the kids so we can celebrate an anniversary with an overnight trip. Those times have been life-giving for us and have created special memories for our kids. It gives Ben and me a much-needed time of focusing on each other instead of the needs of our four children. We can finally have lengthy discussions without interruptions! The practical help of Barb and Ron watching our kids has also allowed us to take a couple of international trips for our ministry. Without their willingness and availability to fly to our home, we would not have had the opportunity to teach and proclaim the gospel in a Muslim nation.

We wish that money and time would allow for us to see Barb and Ron more often. Their generosity to fly each of our kids to spend a special week with them in the summer has been a highlight of the year. We get to spend focused attention with the kids at home, while they enjoy individual time with the others. Now, your involvement in your DIL's life may not look exactly like Barb's—every family is different. And Barb is not perfect; she'd never want anyone to see her as some unattainable standard to strive for. I simply share these things to help encourage you: the lessons learned in this chapter and the advice offered—they really *can* bear fruit in a family. I'm seeing it in my own and I'm so grateful!

If you're a mother-in-law, I'd echo Barb and suggest looking for ways you can speak words of life to your daughter-in-law. Even if you disagree with 90 percent of how she does things, look for the 10 percent that you can praise. Pointing out the good will go a long way in building a bridge to her heart. Instead of giving your opinion on things—for example, how the children should be disciplined—wait until you're asked. This will help your daughter-in-law not to feel judged and evaluated. And like Barb has so graciously said, look for ways you can practically serve your daughter-in-law. Being a wife and mom is exhausting. Send a gift card for a meal out, babysit for a date night, or help carpool the kids to their practices. All of these are ways to alleviate your daughter-in-law's burdens while giving of yourself sacrificially.

And a word of caution—be mindful not to show favoritism to your own daughter (if you have one). There is a natural bond between a mother and daughter. After all, you birthed her and raised her from the time she was a tiny newborn in your arms. Because of that bond, it can be easy to unknowingly invest more in her—more communication, more time, more gifts, more attention to her children. These things can build walls in relationships. Ask God to help you love your daughter-in-law like she was your own daughter, with the same grace and mercy that God has shown you.

Help Them See Jesus

While we are on the topic of service, here's a question: What motivates your service? Do you really desire to glorify God or yourself? Many of our inner battles come from a desire to put ourselves first, not Jesus or our loved one. Ask yourself, "Am I willing to be forgotten if it means my DIL might see and grow in Jesus?" None of us wants to be forgotten but ask God to help you trust him and enable you to make your highest aim to help your family enjoy Jesus. Embrace the opportunities God gives you to encourage their faith. Some will take to heart our spiritual lessons only when we first share our lives by serving them.

When Melissa embraced her call as a MIL, she began to pray that God might work through her to grow her family's faith. During the first years of her son and DIL's marriage they lived far apart. But when her twin grandsons were seven years old, the family moved close by. Then the happy event of a new baby made the young family's apartment seem way too small for two active little boys. With no place to play, video games at least kept the kids from waking up the baby. The house was a mess and the boys were out of control. Melissa's DIL was going crazy and called her for help.

Melissa thought about the time involved and wondered if she was ready to care for seven-year-olds. Then she remembered her prayer. She knew it would not be easy. But instead of complaining, she embraced God's opportunity to encourage faith in her family. She looked forward to becoming a hands-on grandma. Melissa arrived and saw the boys either glued to their video games or fighting over their turn. But there was hope. This family followed Christ. And God was with Melissa!

During a fight, Melissa took one of the boys aside and asked, "Do you know why I want to talk with you, Chad?" He quickly shouted, "It's not my fault. I wouldn't have done anything wrong if it hadn't been for Charlie. He's the one to blame, not me." Melissa continued, "Chad, it doesn't help you to try and blame another person for your own actions. I will talk with Charlie too, but it's important for you to be honest—not just with me—but honest with God. He promises forgiveness and mercy when we confess our sin to him. He promises that Jesus paid for all our sins, including this one! Would you like to pray and ask God to forgive your anger and help you share with Charlie?"

Chad replied, "Not right now—maybe later." With grace Melissa continued, "It is a wonderful gift to be forgiven by such a loving heavenly Father. For right now understand that it is my expectation that you obey your Mom and Dad's house rule—no fighting with your brother." After a similar conversation with Charlie, Melissa cheered whenever the boys cooperated. Best of all, Melissa's daughter-in-law, who had overheard the conversations, said she had always wondered how to address discipline issues with the truth of the gospel. Melissa never guessed how God would use this opportunity to not only serve her family in the practical ways, but build up their faith. Never underestimate the opportunities God offers you to serve your DIL—they may be the vehicle by which you point them to the gospel and invest in them spiritually, not just practically.

Along with the power of words, forgiveness, encouragement, and service, here are some final ways every mother-in-law can come alongside her daughter-in-law:

Prayer: You will forge the strongest relationship with your daughter-in-law if your relationship with God is growing. Ask God. He will give you insight into the spiritual battles your daughter-in-law faces. Ask God to help you remember the hard places you endured in the early years of marriage. Pray for her as you wish someone had prayed for you. Unexpected words may still hurt. Pressures will come. But as you depend on God, he will give you a way out (1 Cor. 10:13). Ask God to make you more like Jesus. Use Scripture as a springboard for prayer. You might begin by praying for yourself and your daughter-in-law with Philippians 2:1–16a open before you.

Forgive the past: *Wait, didn't we already talk about forgiveness?* Yes! And there's a reason it's listed in this chapter twice: because of all the barriers between MIL and DIL, unforgiveness is the strongest! We all need constant reminders to forgive. Has she hurt you? Has she wounded you? Ask God for a heart to forgive any slights. Don't wait for her to ask or until you feel like it. Forgive her. Committed love promises forgiveness. Your resentment is a weed in your family's life that chokes out love. Forgiveness kills weeds. Ask her forgiveness when you sense that you have hurt her. Perhaps you have done no wrong, but hedging your apology with "if I hurt you" will only harm your relationship. Unless you humbly repent, self-pity will eat away at your relationship. God is able! Trust him to work out his perfect plan and purpose in her heart. As you repent and forgive, God will teach you to love your in-law for who she is, not for what she will give you (Eph. 4:31–32).

Give your daughter-in-law room to grow: Think of how much you have grown through the years. Your daughter-in-law is learning and growing. She may pick up more from you than you think . . . and more from your example than your words. Don't interrupt or ask prying questions. At first, offer advice only when asked. (Over time, as the relationship becomes established, there may be appropriate time to offer fitting words of counsel here and there. But do the work of establishing the relationship first, and even then, make unsolicited advice the exception instead of the rule.) Don't guilt-trip your daughter-in-law. Manipulation only works in the short term. Kindness thinks the best of others, so give her the benefit of the doubt. Ask God for opportunities to speak sincere words of praise often as she grows over time.

Ask yourself hard questions: Whose feelings do I really hold most dear—hers or mine? What is my motive when I offer to help her clean—to help or insult her? When I know my daughter-in-law's preferences for her kids and sugar, why do I keep giving them candy? Do I want them to love me more than they respect their mother? Will my invitation to come for this summer trip cause tension in their marriage or press their budget too far? Is our extravagant gift an act of love or a bribe? Will my words make her feel secure or defensive? Do I listen to find fault or with a tender heart ready to pray? What do I notice most about her—her strengths or weaknesses?[6]

Consider the future: Do you have vision for what your relationship with your DIL might do for the generations to come? Have you considered that the work you're doing right now with her might have the power to stop the cycle of unhealthy relational patterns that may have been passed down to you? Your relationship with your daughter-in-law is a building block toward that greater vision. Begin now to ask Christ to make your relationship a strong foundation for many faithful generations to come (Isa. 58:12). Your contentment is key. Ask God to help you embrace this season of life as his gift. Let your joy in loving your own husband and others be a model for your daughter-in-law. As Moses did with Joshua, encourage and serve those coming after you. If you had a hard relationship with family members in your past, be the change you wish you would have had, and watch how it impacts the future!

Help! My Daughter-in-Law Does Not Love Jesus

Here's some help for those who read this chapter and long for a different daughter-in-law—one that's a Christian! God does not make mistakes. He puts every family together for a purpose. A mother-in-law can come alongside her unbelieving daughter-in-law for God's glory. Through your prayer, forgiveness, encouragement, and service, God will point your daughter-in-law to Jesus—the one who will meet her every need. Keep obeying God's Word and his call to love her. Keep coming alongside her in grace, even when she doesn't understand it, and yes, even when she hurts you. Your example and love are ways he is showing her a living picture of Christ. She may be blind to him right now, but you are one way God might be helping her see. ✦

Discussion Questions

1. What stands out to you about the role changes for both mother-in-law and daughter-in-law? In what ways do you feel disoriented by the shifting landscape?

2. What are you asking God to do in a tense time you are in with your in-law?

3. This chapter explored the reality of differences. What is the biggest difference between you and your in-law? How might you celebrate that difference instead of feeling annoyed or threatened by it? In what way might that difference help balance you out?

4. What would need to change for you to become an encourager like Moses?

5. Of all the ideas listed in this chapter for coming alongside your in-law, which is most challenging to you? Why? How might you address that weakness in the coming days?

6. Let's get practical. In what ways will you plan to come alongside your in-law in the next month? Who in your life might hold you accountable to this, even when it gets hard?

7. What have you learned about Jesus's service that impacts your in-law relationship?

8. What current stressful situation are you facing with your in-law? How might this be an opportunity to shape your in-law's view of God?

FAITHFUL
EXPRESSIONS

*Appreciating Each Other's
Relationship with God*[1]

My mother-in-law (Rose) and I (Barb) came to our new relationship from different backgrounds. We had an uncomfortable contrast of priorities. I loved to travel and meet new people, while she felt secure at home close to family. Her family members had always found jobs in their hometown. My family had lived in whatever state the best job offers took us. Our most uncomfortable difference surfaced in our different religious backgrounds. Rose's church worship style, so familiar to her, was a foreign language to me. I wondered how everyone knew exactly what to say and do next without a written order of worship. Even the children kept up with the right prayers and gestures at the right time. Did my clueless expression peg me as an unbeliever or just an outsider? I wondered if this religious difference would divide us.

We've explored all sorts of differences between in-laws in this book so far, but in this chapter, we'll give focused attention to the inevitable differences in the way they walk with God.

I Know What's Best for You!

Could you hear the tension in the relationship I had with my mother-in-law? As time went on, it became clear that we both felt strongly about our choices and various Christian convictions. Did we assume our way was best for the other? Probably. Though we both loved God, we easily fell into the trap of judging and criticizing. We saw the faults and weaknesses of each other more easily than we accepted them. Every futile attempt to change the other woman built frustration.

Does this sound familiar? Perhaps it happening in your own relationship with your in-law, or in a friend's relationship with her in-law. After all, many relationships between in-laws are known for backbiting and arguing. Why? We judge our in-law as guilty and sentence them to rejection! Our judgment becomes a reason to ridicule and distance ourselves from each other. It's easy for us to misunderstand, disagree, judge, and reject. What motivates our quick suspicion? If we spotlight our in-law's faults, we will be more likely to forget about our own! We are wise to be aware of our own pride.

In case we forget to consider our biased assessment in contrast to God's perfect justice, Jesus tells us, "Do not judge, so that you won't be judged. For you will be judged by the same standard with which you judge others" (Matt. 7:1–2). Let's remind ourselves to think about God judging us before we judge others in God's family. You might think your in-law is the "weaker sister," but even so, you are to bear with her and leave room for her convictions (1 Cor. 8:11; Rom. 14:1–9; 15:14). Leave God to judge the heart of our believing in-law. Jesus will bring to the light what is now hidden. He alone will reveal and respond to the motives of our hearts (1 Cor. 4:5).

Jesus gave the watching world the right to judge our true belief in him by our love for one another (John 13:35). The Holy Spirit will give us the power to break our habit of tearing each other down. With the Lord's help, we can break out of the world's mold and build each other up in love. Indeed, the mark of Christian love is accepting, receiving, and loving one another.

So how do we love one another? How can we avoid sending the message, "I know what is best for you"? What does love look like amidst differences in our walks with God? Here are some ideas that may help.

1. Love looks like making room for her choice to differ from yours in the places God's Word is not precise.

God's Word is crystal clear about certain things. At the same time, there are a number of things it speaks less precisely on. For example, there's not a verse we can point to when it comes to which Bible study method to use. Or consider attire on a Sunday. We may talk with our in-law about our preferences, but we cannot argue if she wears jeans to church. Furthermore, God's Word does not tell us what church to attend or if we should send our kids to a Christian school. In these sorts of things, we cannot judge another woman of God who makes a different choice. Why are God's people to accept each other? We are to accept each other because we both belong to God! Christians are not free to decide to resent each other. Again, we are to love each other, and where Scripture is not precise, love looks like making room for the convictions of others—yes, even hers—instead of picking a fight or making every conversation an argument.

2. Love looks like respecting your in-law and listening.

In the early years of our relationship, Rose and I engaged more often in debate than conversation—attempting to convince each other of our views. With time and knowing that we both loved God, we moved from judging to respecting each other. Later we gave each other freedom to make choices without criticism. We found peace in knowing that even though we would not agree with each other on many things, we could honor one another.

What happens when in-laws disagree? Young Tara believes God is not pleased when we wear makeup or certain clothes. She was raised to never cut her hair and to cover her head in church. Now she applies these same restrictions to her kids out of fear of today's strong negative peer pressure. Her mother-in-law, Beth, is concerned that Tara is judging others on outward appearance more than faith in Christ. Beth thinks that with a little more Bible study, Tara could depend more on scriptural truth than on outward appearance. Yet Tara assumes the opposite. She thinks her mother-in-law has a lax attitude toward the ways of the world, and hopes that Beth's time in the Word will convince her to be more disciplined and faithful. How do they get to the point of respecting one another?

Listening is one way of conveying respect. Without listening, it's easy to overgeneralize and criticize one another. We so quickly end up defending our thoughts rather than moving toward understanding. Listening leads to understanding. Beth and Tara have the opportunity to ask, "I'm interested in hearing more. Would you like to tell me your thoughts?" Judgment and criticism are less likely when we hear each other's hearts, and being quick to listen offers the chance to genuinely hear the other's point of view without assuming we know it already.

3. Love looks like appreciating the differences and looking for strengths.

Consider this situation. A daughter-in-law's family decided the Saturday night worship service is best for them. They work hard all week. Sunday is the one day to sleep in, clean, grocery shop, and enjoy a movie night together as a family. She and her husband love the relaxed feel of the Saturday service. Lots of local restaurants make after-church fellowship with friends possible, and they could really use encouragement from Christian friends at the end of a long week. The mother-in-law thinks to herself, *Why can't they set aside Sundays for the Lord? It can't be good for the kids to have this casual approach to worship. They would be so much happier if their priorities were right.* It's not hard for the daughter-in-law to read her mother-in-law's judgment of her decision and resent it. How can these women express love instead of judgment?

Or put yourself in Kathryn's story. When Kathryn (daughter-in-law) and her husband married, they made the choice to attend a liturgical church. The familiar order of worship became a basis of comfort and growth. Kathryn knows that the catechism, hymns, and structured Bible study at church have grown her love for God.

Patricia (mother-in-law) thrives in the freedom and spontaneity of the worship service in her non-denominational church. Her church actively supports many community issues. She looks forward each week in participating in her church's prison Bible study. Patricia thinks Kathryn is too tied to tradition. She's afraid she is missing all that God has for her—freedom to worship and follow God's call. Kathryn thinks her mother-in-law Patricia is missing the beauty and riches of God. She's concerned that Patricia is missing the benefit of worshipful structure that tradition provides. Each thinks the other is missing something essential.

Both women love God. Both wonder about the reality of the other's faith. Patricia wonders why her daughter-in-law doesn't do more to help those who can't help themselves. What good is faith if it does not produce good works? How will she teach her children to be good Christians if all they care about is memorizing the catechism answers? Kathryn sees her mother-in-law's failure to diligently practice the spiritual disciplines as laziness. The doctrine at Patricia's church seems a mile wide and an inch deep. If Patricia isn't growing in her relationship with God, do her works come from faith?

Again, both women love God. So why can't they have a conversation without judging each other? Patricia feels less than honest if she doesn't say exactly what she thinks. But more often than not, her "truth telling" stirs up an argument. Kathryn also strives to be transparent. But why are defensive comments always on the tip of her tongue? Like Patricia, her unkind words often provoke anger. Patricia and Kathryn's conversations usually end with both women feeling injured and guilty.

Is division the only option for all these women? What can they do to overcome the resentment festering in their hearts? By not only listening, as mentioned before, they could seek to understand their differences in this season of life. They could consider the other person's situation: "What's her real life like in this season, and what are the convictions God has given her in this stage of her journey?" More times than not, the answer will become clear: *she's being as faithful as she can in her current situation, and she's fighting to honor her convictions.*

This principle of appreciating differences doesn't just apply to which church service to attend. It applies to many diverse issues within the body of Christ. For example, our in-law may have a different view on baptism, or spiritual gifts, or whether a woman should stay at home or work in the marketplace.

The key in all these differences is to respectfully navigate the challenge for the good of the overall relationship. Instead of criticizing, what if we asked God to help us see the godly character traits in our in-law? Instead of judging, what if we asked God to help us appreciate the other woman's strengths? Instead of assuming there's no way one of her beliefs could be any good, what if we looked for the ways her walk with God is bearing fruit in the life of her family and her church? What if we moved from not only making room for one another's differences, but *appreciating* them? I was amazed by God's creativity in working through my relationship with Rose to teach me more about love. Knowing that we both loved God, we moved from judging to appreciating each other's differences. Not only that, but God worked to bring me to the end of myself. As I depended on him for help, I grew to know and love him more deeply.

4. Love looks like searching for commonalities.

What a surprise to find that in all the differences we find similarities. The more we listen, respect and appreciate one another, the more we may be surprised by all we have in common. Of all your differences in the faith category, take some time to consider what you might have in common. A hobby? A favorite movie genre? A favorite book of the Bible? A favorite recipe? A love for ministry? A knack for crafts or exercise or interior design? Love looks like searching out common ground more than you search out dividing lines.

Ultimately, the love of God and love for our family are the greatest commonalities a MIL and DIL can have. No need to waste time arguing about matters that God's Word is either not precise about, or does not address at all. This does not mean that there's not a place for deeply exploring one's own convictions about certain things, or searching the Scriptures for the light it does shed on certain topics. It simply means that we should not shun, berate, or condemn each other when our choices differ. Once again, we are to love each other. We are to accept each other because we both belong to God. He is what unites us—and that will help us make it through the long-haul together.

If Your In-Law Isn't a Christian

So far, we've explored how to come together in the Lord despite differences in our daily Christian practices. But what if you and your in-law don't even have Jesus in common? What if one of you isn't a believer? When an in-law is not a follower of Christ, a relationship can be tense. Perhaps you'll relate to my (Barb) story.

Why did preparing for my mother's visits feel like I was preparing for battle? All these years later, I can still feel the tension that came over me before she arrived. Mom was winsome and lively. My husband and I admired her zest for life. We loved her and wanted our kids to love her, too. But Mom didn't know Jesus. How could we protect our kids from her ungodly influence and at the same time honor our mother and father?

God fulfilled our desire for our kids to love their grandmother. But predictable questions followed every visit: "Why doesn't Grandmom like our church?" "Why does Grandmom use the Lord's name like that?" "Why did she want to watch that bad movie?" "Does Grandmom really not believe in God?"

We longed for our kids to have godly grandparents, but the Lord had other plans. Over time, we learned three important lessons.

God Designs Relationships for His Best Purposes

My mom's role in our family's life was not a mistake. A good God designed this relationship for our good and his glory. God's good plan for families includes every generation. In time we learned to place limits when a child's safety is at stake. I gave my fears increasingly over to God in prayer. As God, not fear, guided me, problems with my mother became divine opportunities to teach my kids biblical truth with grace. My mother continued to choose to believe that this world is all there is and to live apart from God. She had no category for sin, and therefore, no comfort in God's grace for sinners.

In response, I learned to talk openly with our kids. After my mother's visits, I communicated biblical truth to the kids. Not only the truth about their grandmother's sins but also to examine our own struggles with impatience, self-righteousness, and fear. Along with our kids, we learned that God doesn't wait until we do right to pour out his grace on us. Their grandmother's poor choices could not change their love for her. God softened my heart with compassion for my mother's blindness and ignorance. Her visits still made me tense. But our relationship became an opportunity for spiritual growth. To my surprise, I loved my mother more, not less, after her visits.

In Christ, We Can Be Honest and Confident in Any Relationship

As time went on, God increased my confidence in him. My mother's towering presence in our lives no longer intimidated me. I learned to say, "Yes, Grandmom says that. We love her, but her way of talking does not honor God." Or, "Your Grandmother doesn't believe in Jesus. But we know that everything God tells us about Jesus is true." Acknowledging the problem of unbelief helped my children learn to live wisely within their own family. Anything less would be dishonest and unloving.

Gradually the questions the kids asked after my mother's visits no longer threw me. Instead of changing the subject, I seized the opportunity to help my kids think about their grandmother's unbelief biblically. As God's Word and Spirit guided, my confidence grew. I learned to talk honestly with my children and at the same time avoid sinful criticism. My rule became: Let Mom be who she is, and let our children know her just as the person she is.

Would life have been easier had Mother lived her life the same way we did? Of course. In a perfect world, it would've been great if her example reinforced Christian ideals to our kids. Even so, a Christian mother need not fear. God has entrusted to her and her husband the greatest influence over their children. He will help them seize teachable moments to instruct their kids with honesty and confidence, and he will also give them the power to speak respectfully but firmly to their parents about how they intend to parent.

Living by Faith Honors Our Elders and Requires Us to Lay Down Our Rights

My mother's idea of Christmas was just about Santa. He always showed up during our Christmas visit. What was I to do? First Corinthians 8:9 (NIV) reminds us: "Be careful, however, that the exercise of your rights does not become a stumbling block to the weak." When a biblical imperative wasn't at stake, I honored my mother by setting aside my own preferences.

To stumble means to trip or fall. We honor our in-laws by taking obstacles out of their path. When a command of God is

not at stake, what happens when we demand our own way? We become the obstacle in our in-law's path to their knowing the love of God in Christ. When we stick to demanding our rights, how can we pretend to be acting in love? God commands us to show love and compassion to those who do not yet know him. We deny our own desires for the sake of others because that is what Jesus has done for us.

We couldn't agree with my mother about many things, but I could honor her even as we disagreed. I could tell my mom, "I don't think it's fair for the kids to hear this," or, "Watching that movie in front of the kids could confuse them about right and wrong." As much as possible, I privately asked my mom to do things our way.

Living by faith meant that I couldn't push my mother aside simply because she didn't believe what we did. God graciously taught me how to let go of the small stuff. God developed my ability to discern between his commands and my preferences, and wherever I could, prefer my mother over myself.

How do we live with an unbelieving in-law? Fear of your in-law's influence may try to keep you from entering fully into God's purposes for your family. Their choices may continue to grieve you. Ask God to replace your fear with faith in his plan. He does not leave it up to you to change your in-law. He does not promise that every unbelieving in-law will believe. But God will work through your life—many times without your awareness—to do what only he can do. He will use your example to be a signpost of who Christ is, and what he is like.

God's Invitation

We can all fall prey to criticizing one another's walk with God (or lack thereof). What can we do to mend a relationship

broken by this? Every in-law relationship is God's invitation to lessen the hold our sin has on us. I can attest to this! My (Barb) relationship with Stacy has revealed many of my blind spots. Several times I have needed to ask myself, "Will I let go of having to be right?" On more than one occasion I would have been wise to ask for Stacy's forgiveness. But one time in particular, while we waited at the airport to say good-bye, God prompted me to ask her, "Have I done anything to offend you?" and then, "Please forgive me."

So when the day is over and you rehearse a conversation with your in-law that did not go well, what do you do? Most of us ask God to forgive us and then go back to sleep. Let me suggest a plan for the next day.

- Ask God for grace and courage to go to your in-law. Pride and anger will fight you on the need to confess your sin. But God says we are to confess our sins to him and to one another—even if it seems to us that our in-law is 90 percent responsible (1 John 1:5–10).
- Ask God to show you the way to enter into these hard conversations. We are not to shift the blame to our in-law, even if she has sinned. We are not to use words or questions to avoid taking responsibility. Instead, we seriously consider our own sin first and show the example of taking responsibility for our part in what went wrong.
- Ask God to help you say, "I was wrong. Please forgive me." It's so easy to fall into the trap of not really apologizing. Instead we say, "I'm sorry" or "If I've done anything to offend

you" which takes no responsibility for what happened.

- Ask God to loosen the hold sin has on you. Self-righteousness will resist you on the road to change. To fight it, start asking, "Are there ways I can better show you my love and respect?" as a sign of your humble intent. You'd be surprised how much it not only softens your own heart, but the heart of your in-law. Guards will come down.

Our many differences in our Christian walk can divide the in-law relationship fairly fast. Comparisons stir up pride and envy. Judgments and criticisms cut deep, creating lasting wounds. God tells us that when we cling to having to have our own way, we don't know where we are going—"the darkness has blinded his eyes" (1 John 2:11). Yet God invites us out of that darkness and into his light with the tools of respect, appreciation, commonalities, and grace, even for those who may not know him yet. May we come together in his name, showing the world around us just how powerfully unifying our God is! ✒

Discussion Questions

1. Which story in this chapter spoke to you the most?

2. What is the biggest difference between your walk with God and your in-law's?

3. When have you found it hard to accept your in-law's choices or convictions?

4. How do you typically respond when you and your in-law disagree on something convictional?

5. Can you describe a time when God gave you strength to deny yourself instead of demanding your own way? How might that memory give you faith for your current disagreement with your in-law?

6. What are the three ways this chapter recommends for handling our differences in love? Which of those is hardest for you? Why?

7. Consider the section in this chapter that describes how to handle an in-law who does not know the Lord. What stands out to you most? How does this section encourage you? How does it challenge you?

SUFFERING TOGETHER

Supporting Each Other in the Midst of Pain

Barb, please pray for us. There is so much angst, blame and division. My heart is heavy for the burden Ben is carrying."

Ministry is rough. When I (Stacy) was a young, starry-eyed seminary wife, I had only the biggest and best dreams for our future life of ministry—a fruitful and growing church, good friends, grateful congregants who would appreciate my husband's preaching and teaching. And in some ways, God has given us many of those desires. Our children have grown up in our church, and many of the members seem like extended family. They've celebrated birthdays, piano recitals, and soccer games with us, filling in for our blood family who are hundreds of miles away. Friendships have deepened as we've walked beside people experiencing intense suffering. We're grateful for our church and the friends God has provided to serve alongside us.

But with it has come manifold heartaches—issues of church discipline, disagreements over various decisions, investing time and energy into members who then leave when a need isn't met. When a difficult or unpopular decision is made by the elders, I've lost friendships. It's one of the most sobering parts of being in full-time ministry.

It's times like these that I pick up my phone and call my mother-in-law. One of the biggest bonding agents in our relationship has been Barb's care and concern for our family during trials. We shoot texts back and forth with our immediate needs and concerns. We pray Scripture for each other and bolster one another with the Word of God. It's an incredible privilege to have a praying mother-in-law, and I don't take it for granted.

Life Is Full of Trials

In Elisabeth Elliot's classic book *Keep a Quiet Heart*, she reminds us, "When Paul and Silas were in prison, they prayed and sang. It isn't troubles that make saints, but their response to troubles."[1]

Maybe you're reading this book and you're in the prime of your life. You're preparing for your wedding and imagine a picture-perfect life and family. It can be hard to think of life being filled with trials! But Christians are not exempt from troubles. In fact, we're promised troubles for the very fact that we follow Christ (John 15:20). Yet often, our responses to the trials in our lives reveal that we think we deserve something better.

- We're looked over for a promotion and automatically think the worst of our bosses and the seemingly unqualified person who got the job instead. *I've served you all these years, God—why won't you give me the glory and the paycheck I deserve?*

- Or we're mocked for our faith in the work-place and respond with resentment—toward our coworkers as well as the God who seemed to let us down. *I've been so faithful, God—why not give me favor here? Why won't you guarantee me a place in the in-crowd? They're the real bad guys—they defame your name all the time! Why give them the close friendships?*

- Or we're not treated with the love and affec-tion we think we deserve from our mother-in-law or daughter-in-law. *What's wrong with her? Why the coldness? I've done everything right!*

- Even in the battle with infertility, instead of receiving God's comfort, mercy, and help in our sorrow, we can raise our fist at God, interrogating him on why he blessed others with multiple children while we're left with empty arms. *Who is she that you'd give her a child and not me? I've followed all the steps and rules and orders from the doctors! I've checked all the boxes and I've prayed all the right prayers. And yet you withhold!*

We're talking about trials far more severe than a rained-out picnic. And yet, even here, complaints of soggy sandwiches and park-side puddles reveal our sinful sense of entitlement toward having our "rights" fulfilled. And when we don't get them, we can have our own temper tantrums in a hundred different ways. In trials big and small, instead of running straight into God's consolation, lifting up a cry for his mercy and strength, we often dart down the well-worn path of resentment and bit-terness, carrying a club.

Rejoicing to Share with Christ

While the path of shock, entitlement, resentment, or bitterness is the world's way of handling a trial, the apostle Peter exhorts us to respond to the difficulties in our lives in a completely foreign and countercultural way: "Dear friends, don't be surprised when the fiery ordeal comes among you to test you, as if something unusual were happening to you. Instead, rejoice as you share in the sufferings of Christ, so that you may also rejoice with great joy when his glory is revealed" (1 Pet. 4:12–13).

Peter is calling us to have a heavenward focus in this life. Trials will surely come, and we should not be caught off guard. In fact, they're the very thing God uses to test our faith. And we are not just to endure the hardships, but actually rejoice in the very suffering we experience, knowing that through suffering hard things in this life, we taste a small portion of the bitter cup Jesus endured when he was hung on the cross for the sake of our sins. Individual Christian or two in-laws in the Lord, trials shouldn't be shocking. We know God is using this difficulty to shape us to be more like his Son, and in the in-law relationship, we seek to help one another grow into that image.

Be Prepared for Fiery Trials

If we're not to be surprised when difficult things come into our lives, it follows that we should be prepared. Consider six ways to be ready for a trials when it appears in your life or the life of your in-law. Being ready together can help you move through the trial with greater strength.

1. Expect suffering.

Though our world was created by God and he loves it, each time a hardship enters our lives, we're reminded that this world is not in the shape it once was, nor in the shape it will one day be. Right now, it's still fallen. Distorted by sin. We are broken people living in a broken, sin-filled world. If we try to make our lives into some sort of utopia here and now, we'll surely be disappointed. Yes, God will restore and renew all things one day, but that hasn't happened yet. Expect this fallen world to let you down sometimes.

2. Know God's Word.

Fight the fight of faith by studying, meditating on, and treasuring the promises of God's Word. A closed Bible will yield little hope or strength for our journey. Arm yourselves with the sword of the Spirit to fight the battle well, for our battle is spiritual, and requires weapons of the Spirit (Eph. 6:12, 17). (One way to help your in-law be ready for trials is to share Scripture passages at appropriate times, memorize a passage together, or perhaps even join a Bible study together.)

3. Pray for perseverance.

Call upon the only one who can sustain you with grace in the midst of your difficulty. "Pray at all times in the Spirit with every prayer and request, and stay alert with all perseverance and intercession for all the saints" (Eph. 6:18). If your in-law is one of those saints, call upon her! Her prayers are valuable and can help sustain you in seasons of sorrow or testing.

4. Be committed to a body of believers.

God does not mean for us to endure suffering on our own.
When the Israelites were fighting Amalek, they were only victori-
ous as long as Moses was raising up his arms. But he grew weary
in the battle and needed the help of Aaron and Hur to hold up
his arms when he lost strength (Exod. 17:8–13). Who will come
to your aid when the road gets rough? While the majority of
these people should be found in your local church context, it's a
sweet gift to have an in-law who will "hold up your arms" sometimes. How might you hold up the arms of your in-law?

5. Look for reasons to rejoice.

My natural reaction to suffering is to feel sorry for myself
and complain. But when I can catch myself heading down that
downward spiral, I combat it with making a simple list of five
things to be grateful for. Remembering God's blessings can
help us keep the right perspective, even in the midst of hardships. (And if you're looking to grow in gratitude, invite your
in-law along. Reach out when you are having a hard time being
thankful. Ask her to remind you of sweet memories and times
the Lord has been good to you.)

6. Keep doing good.

Suffering can make us self-absorbed. We might tend to
think that no one's lot is as difficult as our own. But Peter
exhorts us that in the midst of our trial, we need to stay others-
focused: "So then, let those who suffer according to God's will
entrust themselves to a faithful Creator while doing what is
good" (1 Pet. 4:19).[2]

Suffering does not exempt us from doing good for others.
Keep reaching out, keep praying for others, keep looking for

SUFFERING TOGETHER

ways to bless and encourage someone else in the midst of their difficult time.

What if the person enduring suffering is your mother-in-law or daughter-in-law? How might God be using the trials in life to draw you together in unity? The trials of ministry and the heartaches of parenting are ways the Lord opened up communication between Barb and me. I know that she is a trusted friend and counselor, someone I can share my heart with who will not only listen but seek the Lord alongside me. Over the years, trust has been built as I've seen her keep confidences, point me to the truths of Scripture, and listen without judging. She has been a steady source of support and encouragement.

But what if your in-law relationship isn't in this place yet? What if she is not someone you can trust with your heartaches? What if your DIL has resisted your attempts to comfort her in her sorrow? Or your MIL has made you feel more judged than encouraged during difficult days? Suffering presents a fresh opportunity to reach out to those in need of help. The hardest hearts can be softened when they're ministered to during suffering. Even if your past attempts at building a relationship have been ill-received, don't let that stop you from reaching out anew. Try another time to bear the trial together. Nothing bonds people together like a common struggle or battle. Regardless which party is facing the trial right now, reach out to her.

Follow the Ultimate Example

> "For this is what the Lord GOD says: See, I myself will search for my flock and look for them." (Ezek. 34:11)

163

You may sense a hesitation to bear a trial alongside your in-law. You may feel fear in reaching out. Whatever the reason behind that hesitation, consider Jesus. Jesus didn't shy away from messy, hard situations. Instead, he moved toward them. The Lord pursued us even while we were his enemies (Rom. 5:10). We're only capable of love because he first loved us (1 John 4:19). The love and grace he extends to us, we can extend to our in-law.

Jesus sets the example in moving toward difficult people. Think about the parable of the lost sheep from Luke 15:3–7. Even when losing just one of his 100 sheep, the shepherd stops what he is doing to pursue the lost lamb. This is how the Lord pursues us in our sin and rebellion. He cares enough to go after a single lost and hurting lamb. The lamb has done nothing to deserve the shepherd's tender care; in fact, it should probably be scolded for wandering from the fold. The shepherd doesn't shame or scold, but is delighted when that lamb returns to his tender care.

Think about the Samaritan woman who had five husbands (John 4:1–42). Jesus broke the rules of society by traveling through Samaria, speaking with a woman who was entrenched in sin and was despised by the culture. As one thinker puts it, "He pursued this outcast woman, engaged in the longest recorded conversation in the New Testament, and revealed himself to her as the Christ. He came close to her as a servant, friend and God. Our help, in response, is personal. We are a composite of a servant and friend who, as servant, places a priority on the interests of others, and, as friend, enters in, enjoys the person, bears burdens, and even shares what is on our own hearts."[3]

Your God moves toward you in your worst moments. In your hardest moments. In your scariest moments. In the moments you don't deserve him to. What kind of love! Let that love fuel you to move toward your in-law during a season of trial, even if it seems like she doesn't deserve it.

In all of this, there is a question that lingers: What if your biggest trial *is* your in-law?

A Story of Redemption

Brenda candidly shared with me her own story. She has been married for thirty-five years to her husband, John. But from day one, she's had a difficult relationship with her mother-in-law, Marilyn. When John first took Brenda home to meet his parents, it was obvious they were disappointed that she was working instead of pursuing college. "What are your plans for the future?" Marilyn asked her with questioning eyes. It seemed working as a bank teller wasn't exactly what she had in mind for her future daughter-in-law. The wedding added more fuel to the fire when Brenda and John opted for a small, inexpensive wedding with only close friends and immediate relatives. Marilyn had dreamed of inviting friends from every sphere of life and having a grand party at their country club. A simple reception in the church fellowship hall proved utterly disappointing. Within the first week of their marriage, Marilyn shared with Brenda how disappointed she was in the wedding events. "I wish I never came" she told Brenda bitterly.

It was a rocky start to a new relationship. Even though Brenda and John lived only thirty minutes from Marilyn and her husband, the tension between them made the visits fewer and fewer. Brenda constantly felt judged by her mother-in-law, from how she was raising her children to the color of paint on her walls. Family holidays at Marilyn's house were tense, the children never knowing whether they would be reprimanded for being too loud or touching something fragile.

"My husband's family was very distant and unaffectionate. When we would walk in the house at Christmas, no one came to greet us or give us a hug. There were no 'I'm happy to see you! Or 'so glad you're here!'" The hurt feelings intensified when Brenda routinely saw pictures of only one side of the family on display in Marilyn's living room. What happened to the school photos and family Christmas card that she mailed year after year? Eventually, Brenda wondered what might happen if *she* became the host for the holidays. Then she could set the tone for the atmosphere.

"I decided I would treat my in-laws the way I wished that I was treated. I welcomed them at the door with a warm smile and a hug. I told them how happy I was to have them. Over time Marilyn softened and began to return the hugs and greetings. But the real test came five years ago when my father-in-law was diagnosed with cancer and passed away. I knew I needed to step in and help. Marilyn was old and couldn't handle things by herself. She didn't know how to drive and was dependent on others. I started to go over to her house three times each week to take her to her appointments, shop for groceries, and help with things around the house. She seemed grateful that I kept coming over to help. Marilyn was pleasant and stopped grumbling and accusing me of things. It seemed like she even looked forward to talking with me."

Brenda's difficult relationship with Marilyn lasted for decades. Things didn't improve, but seemed to get worse, when children arrived on the scene. Yet that didn't stop Brenda from serving her MIL during intense suffering. When I asked Brenda what made her overlook years of offenses to serve her MIL, she replied, "Since Jesus has freely forgiven my sins and poured out his grace on my life, how can I not do the same for my MIL?"

By the grace of God, Brenda was able to persevere through years of hurt to minister to Marilyn during the most devastating season of her life. The model of Christ's unconditional love and grace spurred Brenda on to loving Marilyn in word and deed. God used the trials of life to soften both the hearts of Marilyn and Brenda toward each other.

Serve in the Strength That God Provides

After so many years of difficulty, how did Brenda find the strength to not return evil with evil, but with a blessing instead?

Just as a car needs fuel to run, so our hearts need fuel to serve those in need. Feasting on the Word of God is essential to keeping our hearts healthy. We'll quickly run out of steam, and hope, if we're waking up day after day with a closed Bible. Our own vain attempts to meet the needs of our suffering in-law will likely result in bitterness and exhaustion when we're not tethered to God's Word.

John 15:5 reminds us, "I am the vine; you are the branches. The one who remains in me and I in him produces much fruit, because you can do nothing without me."

My tomato plants are a sorry sight this fall. Through the brutal heat of the summer, and lack of water due to a negligent gardener, the leaves withered and the vines split. The fledgling cherry tomatoes are still green and falling off the drooping stems. They've been severed from their source of nutrients necessary for life.

In much the same way, we will wither and die apart from the regular intake of God's Word. We abide in Jesus through dwelling on his words as the Holy Spirit convicts us of sin and teaches us. But to dwell on his Word, we must open his Word. We don't read it with a legalistic bent to check off our box, but to commune with God and gain the necessary strength to serve with joy and gratitude.[4] As we dwell on the sacrifice Christ made for sinners like us, we're reminded of the reason we sacrifice for others. Our hope isn't in an easy, comfortable life but in giving our lives away for the sake of the gospel. Memorizing and meditating on God's Word provides hope in the midst of despair, and gives fresh energy to walking alongside our suffering in-law.

> As a deer longs for flowing streams, so I long
>   for you, God.
> I thirst for God, the living God.
> When can I come and appear before God?
>   (Ps. 42:1–2)

Ask God to help your soul long for his Word, his presence. And take comfort in the fact that the Spirit is at work, interceding for you with groans that words cannot express. Lean into the Lord's strength as you serve your in-law. He is using you to reach out to her. His Spirit moving toward her through your arms. And he will be faithful to provide all that you need. "And God is able to make every grace overflow to you, so that in every way, always having everything you need, you may excel in every good work" (2 Cor. 9:8).

Suffering Well Together

Jenny and Susan have one of the sweetest in-law relationships that I've seen. Jenny married Susan's son at the young age of twenty-three. She was a new Christian, and not being raised in a Christian home, often called Susan for biblical advice. Not long into their marriage, Jenny and her husband began to experience significant trials. A miscarriage was followed by years of infertility, failed adoptions, job loss, and a ten-year season of waiting for children. Through all of the heartache, Susan stood beside Jenny and encouraged her with love and support. Jenny told me, "She welcomed me into the family as a daughter, not a daughter-in-law. Susan treats me the same way she treats her own daughter. Throughout our years of waiting for children she prayed for me, cried with me, encouraged me with Scripture and sent small gifts to let me know she was thinking of me. We now live in different states and it seems like absence has made my heart grow fonder. I cry every time they visit and have to leave."

Walking through suffering beside your in-law provides a tangible way to show the love of Christ. But how do we do that? What are the practical ways we can show love and care to a hurting soul?

1. Take a genuine interest in their welfare (Phil. 2:20).

Spend time really getting to know your in-law. What makes them tick? What do they enjoy? How are they struggling? When we take a genuine interest in someone else's welfare, we're more interested in knowing and serving them than in what we can receive from the relationship.

A seasoned pastor's wife gave me this sage advice at the start of our ministry, "Ask good questions. Most people love to talk about themselves and their interests . . . and would much rather talk than listen." So we draw them out and notice what excites them, what fears they have and how we can help them. And we share openly about our own lives—both our joys and struggles. A deeper bond will form when we not only ask good questions, but share our own hearts.

2. Listen well.

When the Israelites were suffering under the yoke of slavery in Egypt, they cried out to the Lord for help: "The Israelites groaned because of their difficult labor, they cried out, and their cry for help because of the difficult labor ascended to God. God heard their groaning, and God remembered his covenant" (Exod. 2:23–24). God is not some far-off being who has no idea what's happening in our lives. He is a personal God, who is close to the hurting. He hears our cries for help and delights to answer them. In Psalm 62:8, we're exhorted to pour out our hearts before God. He is our refuge, and hears the cries of our hearts.

In a similar way, we can be a refuge for our in-law by hearing them—by learning to listen well. We ask good questions, make eye contact, and put our phones away. Instead of thinking about what we'll say, we listen intently to our in-law's words and are slow to respond. We follow the advice of James 1:19 being quick to hear, slow to speak, and slow to anger. Listening well shows that we're truly interested in knowing their heart, not pushing our agenda.

3. Show compassion.

Maybe this seems like an obvious point, but it's easy to be hardened to the pain of others. Sometimes this is because we are in a sinful season where we only think of ourselves first— how someone else's hardship will affect us. When we hear that our mother-in-law is sick, we automatically think about how she won't be able to babysit for our anniversary date. Or when your daughter-in-law shares that the family will be visiting her parents this Christmas, instead of praying for the trip and the chaos the couple will have to handle while they are braving the holidays, we only lament how lonely we'll be around the dinner table. Other times we are hardened to the pain of others because there is some sort of pain we haven't processed in our own lives. We closed ourselves off years ago because of some past hurt that has nothing to do with our in-law and their current trial, and we find that in the moment they need us, we are too calloused to feel their sorrow and respond in tenderness.

Yet God calls us to a different path, one paved with loving compassion. Psalm 103:13 tells us, "As a father has compassion on his children, so the LORD has compassion on those who fear him." The tender, protective love that a father demonstrates to his child is the same compassion that God shows to us. Jesus's time alone on the mountain was inconvenienced by a demanding crowd following him on foot. But his compassion on the crowd moved him away from comfort and toward need—healing those who were sick (Matt. 14:14).

We show compassion to our in-law by showing up, sitting with them in their suffering, and empathizing with their hurts. We look for ways to serve them and alleviate their burdens. Maybe it's making a meal for them when they're sick, or relieving them for the weekend so they can get away and tend to their heart and spend some time with God for a few days. We're promised to have trouble in this world (John 16:33), and we could all use someone in our corner, providing a constant stream of comfort and support.

4. Point out evidence of grace.

In the midst of their pain, watch for reasons to rejoice. Do you see any fruit of the Spirit evident in their life during this hard time—love, joy, peace, patience, kindness, goodness, faithfulness, gentleness, or self-control (Gal. 5:22–23)? Tell them what you see! Suffering can lead us down a lonely path of discouragement. We need others in our lives to point out how they see God working in the midst of our pain. Have you seen your in-law be patient with a trying child?

Tell them. Have you seen them seeking the Lord during a time of grief? Say so! Have they striven to stay joyful or content amid persecution or uncertainty or exhaustion? Let them know. Or what about their steadfast commitment to their local church, showing up for worship when you know they don't feel like showing up? If you see this, encourage them with it; it can help bolster their faith. Walking with your in-law through difficulty provides countless ways to rejoice with those who rejoice and weep with those who weep (Rom. 12:15).

5. Pray.

The most helpful thing we can do for our suffering in-law is bring them before the throne of grace. As we draw out their hearts, listen carefully and show loving compassion, we point them to our ultimate hope.

> I lift my eyes toward the mountains. Where
>   will my help come from?
> My help comes from the LORD, the Maker of
>   heaven and earth. (Ps. 121:1–2)

As our in-law shares their suffering with us, we don't need to have all the answers. Instead, we point them to the truth of God's Word and pray for healing, strength, and God's comfort in their lives. Praying together is intimate. It moves your relationship to a deeper level.

If at first praying together seems awkward, ask for specific ways you can pray for your in-law. Report back to them verses you prayed for them or the words you used. Or if they send you a prayer request via text, go a step beyond "I'll be praying" and type out the prayer right then and there, so they can see the prayer you lifted to God for them in that moment, even though you couldn't be together in person. It may just so happen that they return back to that text for comfort and support later. Or consider asking follow-up questions to their prayer requests: "How did your test go?" "Are you having more time with the kids?" "Is your knee feeling better?"

Following up on prayer requests can mean a lot to the one who vulnerably shared their need. Hearts are softened as you pray God's blessings over each other's lives. "The LORD is near all who call out to him, all who call out to him with integrity" (Ps. 145:18).

Rejoice in Hard Things

Maybe you are blessed right now to be in a sunny season of life, far from trials. If so, be grateful and praise God. But also know that trials will one day enter your life, or the lives of those you love, and are the very means God uses to mold us into his image. The suffering your in-law is experiencing provides a means for you to reach out and show the love of Christ. And the same is true for you—if you happen to be the one suffering, invite your in-law into the burden so you can learn to bear the burden together and grow deeper in relationship than you've ever been before. Whether you're facing trials now, preparing for the trials that will eventually come, or walking your in-law through a trial, rejoice, knowing that through every hard thing we suffer in life, we share with Christ. ✐

Discussion Questions

1. What trials have you experienced in life?

2. What is a meaningful way that someone ministered to you in the midst of your suffering? How might God be preparing to do the same for your in-law?

3. In this chapter, we explored how Scripture exhorts us when we experience trials. Which teaching encouraged you most? Challenged you most?

4. In what ways are you prepared for suffering? In what ways are you unprepared sometimes?

5. This chapter offered many ways in-laws might come alongside each other in suffering. Which of these ideas seems like a good next step for you and your in-law?

6. How might walking through hardships with your in-law serve to strengthen your relationship?

7. Sometimes we are hardened to the trials of our in-law due to sin or past pain. Which of these is most often the culprit for your lack of compassion? To develop compassion, consider the life of your in-law in this season—what are some sorrows or struggles that God is opening your eyes to?

GOING FORWARD
IN LOVE

Choosing to Love Despite the Cost

Ron and I (Barb) had coasted through our first four years of married life. With grad school finished, Ron's first real job had started. Just in time! Now, with the medical insurance we had never worried about before, we could cover the expenses of our first baby. But how could I be a mother? I didn't know the first thing about caring for a child. The thought of holding and feeding a baby scared me. Could I go from being a carefree twenty-four-year-old to caring for the needs of a newborn? Where would I find the love needed to nurture this little human being?

My fears lessened somewhat when I joined a young mom's group. Cheryl, the group's leader welcomed me right away. Did this confident, experienced mom really have it all together? Could her love for her five children be as real as it seemed? Over time, as I watched and listened to Cheryl, I knew the answer was, yes! I learned something much more important from Cheryl than I had expected. Even more than how to be a mom, Cheryl taught me about God. I had never heard that God made me to have a relationship with himself.

Cheryl gave me the bad news about myself as well. She said that sin had broken my (and every person's) relationship with God. Only God could fix my brokenness. He loved me, Barbara, so much that he sent his only Son Jesus to pay the penalty for my sin. Amazingly so, he would forgive me and make me God's child. That loving relationship with him would be mine, not just that day, but forever.

Then I learned that God's greatest commandment is to love him with all our heart, soul, mind, and strength. And we are to love others as we love ourselves. Such an awe-inspiring assignment! But with dashed hopes, I discovered I couldn't— not even for a single day. I had thought becoming a Christian was going to make my life easier. Then I realized this was not God's idea for saving me. Love is so hard. Why did God command me to do the impossible? As I prayed and struggled, I only saw more of my sin. I loved who I wanted to love and not the people I would rather not deal with.

I had no place to go except God. Only he could give me the strength to forgive and love. Relationships are hard. Love isn't easy. And God is the relationship expert we all need. You don't have a lot of choice about your in-law. But once the marriage vows are made, this is the in-law you have in spite of your choice to love.

Not one of the people in my life is there by accident. And that is true for you too. But here's good news—God puts people in our lives for his good purposes. I've said that before, I know, but it bears repeating because we forget it so often. *God has a plan for every relationship.* In fact, God's plan for every relationship is redemption. If you are God's child, trust that he gives you an opportunity to show the power of the gospel through every relationship he gives you. Your relationship with your in-law, whether they know Christ or not, is a platform to show the beauty and power of his Son.

The kind of love I needed was not something that came naturally. The kind of love I needed was God's love. Love is a fruit of the Holy Spirit. Chapters 5 and 7 mentioned 1 Corinthians 13. These verses sound great at a wedding, or on Valentine's Day. Many of us know the words, but how do we live them? I already had the ground knowledge that if I didn't have love I had nothing.

I knew how to love my job, a walk in the park, and ice cream. I knew how to act loving when I wanted something in return. I was used to the evidence of envy, boasting, and arrogance in my conversations. I didn't think I was easily offended, but I was. And instead of admitting my failure, I was more comfortable looking to see what others were doing wrong. But I did not know the nature of biblical love—the kind that engages in loving acts of kindness, compassion, and affection, no matter the response or the cost. What does God say about the love he would grow in my heart not only for my child, but eventually, for my one-day daughter-in-law?

> Love is patient, love is kind. Love does not envy, is not boastful, is not arrogant, is not rude, is not self-seeking, is not irritable, and does not keep a record of wrongs. Love finds no joy in unrighteousness but rejoices in the truth. It bears all things, believes all things, hopes all things endures all things. Love never ends. . . . Now these three remain: faith, hope, and love—but the greatest of these is love. (1 Cor. 13:4–8, 13)

Love Is Patient

Patient people wait for others to catch up because they know how much it hurts to be left behind. Patience doesn't mean quietly seething or stoically gritting your teeth. Patience trusts God. We know God is working. Love for him fuels our patience. We choose to lay aside our own schedule and follow his. Patience keeps frustration from harming our relationships. To be patient is to be like Jesus. Therefore, Scripture commands us both to put on the Lord Jesus (Rom. 13:14) and to put on patience (Col. 3:12). God strengthens us so that we can practice patience. However impossible it may seem, God enables us to do what he commands.[1]

In your in-law relationship, what does this mean? It means this: *wait on her*. If she's behind, if she's struggling, if she's not where you think she should be, wait and pray. God has developed you slowly over the long haul, always patient with you along the way. Embody this in your posture toward her. God is working in her at his own pace—don't try to rush it or point out where she's not fast enough. Let her story unfold according to God's timing.

Love Is Kind

Kindness is more than the nice feeling of a one-time act offered to strangers. Kind people have learned from their own pain and want to extend to others the kindness God has shown them (2 Cor. 1:3–7). So kind people watch for ways to help others. They know how it feels to be forgotten. Kindness with your in-law may mean responding gently to her outrageous insult. Or it might mean choosing to allow her needs to rewrite our to-do list. Kindness does not demand that she must appreciate our sacrifices. This kind of kindness does not come naturally. Is it any wonder that Scripture must command us to put on kindness (Col. 3:12)?

Look at our Savior. Jesus looked not only to his own interests, but also to the interests of others (Phil. 2:4). When we obey God's command to be kind, we are like Jesus. Our kindness comes from him.

Love Does Not Envy

Love does not crave what someone else has. Not only are loving people grateful for what God has given, but they rejoice in how God has blessed others. Love does not work hard to get things for itself. Because loving people are content with what they have, they can turn their focus from themselves to meet the needs of others. The Bible tells us what we have all learned by painful experience—envy destroys (Prov. 14:30; James 3:14–16). Envy is an issue of the heart (Mark 7:20–23). None of us can solve that heart problem on our own. God has given us a Savior who has saved us from our empty way of life that loved ourselves above others. In him, we are free to put aside envy which only destroys others and loves ourselves (1 Pet. 1:18–2:2). In Christ alone we have the power of the Holy Spirit to strengthen us in our fight with sin (Gal. 2:20).

What does this mean with our in-law? Loving means throwing off any covetous thoughts: If only we had the money they did. Or It would have been nice in my child-rearing years to have all the gadgets she has—what a breeze that would have been! Or Well of course she's chipper—her world is so easy in her stage of life. Her life doesn't require her to be up all night with a screaming toddler! I wish I had her time—and her sleep. Or Look at her fancy job. I wish God would have given me better options as a mom back when I was trying to make my way in the world.

Those kinds of thoughts only create wedges and if left to breed over time, they will destroy the relationship. God gave your in-law the life he gave her, and he gave you the life he gave you. The details differ, but he gives us each what we need to learn and grow. She has her lot, and you have yours, and God didn't make a mistake. He's not holding out on you. There's no need for envy—God is good to you.

Love Is Not Boastful / It Is Not Arrogant

Loving people do not brag or attempt to put others down (1 Cor. 4:6, 18–19; 5:2; 8:1). They don't waste time trying to get others to notice their possessions or titles. Loving people reject the need to defend themselves. Pride breaks relationships. Love brings peace to broken relationships. Love follows Jesus, who humbled himself when he came to bring us his peace (Phil. 2). Jesus died and rose from the dead to make peace between us and God (Rom. 5:1). He gave himself to restore our broken relationship with God (Eph. 2:14–15). Do you know the joy of a restored relationship with God? If so, God calls you to make the first move in restoring broken relationships. Gospel humility demands we work hard to strengthen the relationships God gives us. In Christ we can do even what seems impossible.[2]

For our in-law, this means that we put off any form of pride in our relationship. We do not need to overtly rattle off all we've done or accomplished in front of her to garner praise or prove our worth. Nor should we do this in subtle ways, dropping in passive-aggressive statements that draw attention to our efforts. Because we are seen and valued by God, we don't need to brag in order to receive the validation of our in-law. Instead, we can praise!

Love Is Not Rude, Is Not Self-Seeking, Keeps No Record of Wrongs

Instead of only pursuing the needs of self, love pays attention to the needs of others. Loving people do not grow resentful when others fail to pay attention to them. Selfishness and rudeness grow side by side. Consider this with your in-law: Do you enjoy the laughs that your sharp or sarcastic words receive so much that you ignore how they might hurt her? What do your condescending comments say about your need to build yourself up? How often do you dredge up past failures in order to maintain control? Love for God and others shows that we are God's child (1 John). Jesus does not tell us that loving ourselves is wrong. Instead he says that the love we have for others must equal the concern we commonly have for ourselves (Mark 12:30–31).[3]

When we operate according to this biblical wisdom, we'll find we're walking in love. We'll find that we don't have time to keep records of our in-law's mistakes—we're too busy recalling all the things she's gotten right!

Love Finds No Joy in Unrighteousness but Rejoices in the Truth

Loving people choose truth when lies might seem to make life easier. Love does not try to get away with bad behavior or take consolation when that perfect person messes up. Loving people rejoice in the truth that God does not ignore our sin just because he loves us. God's great love provides the way for our sins to be forgiven, in Christ (1 John 4:10). The right response to sin, whether our own or another's, is sadness. Loving people rejoice in the truth that though we are sinful, Jesus loves us. In him we can love the imperfect people God calls us to love. With our in-law, this means that we mourn if there is some lie she is believing, and we do what we can to model and speak the truth.

Love Bears All Things, Believes All Things, Hopes All Things, Endures All Things

Loving people believe the best of others and give them the benefit of the doubt. Loving people persevere when they feel like giving up on others. They depend on Jesus's strength to love, not on themselves. Loving people do not delude themselves with wishful thinking, yet they look ahead to better days. They rest on the fact that God has sent his Spirit to work out his will in his people (Phil. 2:12b–13; 3:14). The costly love God calls us to, hurts. But God does not give up on us, so we do not give up on others when trials and hardships come (1 Pet. 1:5–8). For our in-law, this means that we always hold out hope that God can move, no matter how bleak the situation looks. It means that we bear the rough patches in the strength of the Lord, and endure the stormy seasons in the relationship with fortitude, believing that God will use it for our good, her good, and his glory.

Removing the Log Makes Room for Love

I'll never forget the conversation. I'd been a mother-in-law for all of one year. Now a church friend was looking to me as someone with great experience. Her son's wedding was right around the corner. My friend hated the thoughts and feelings swirling around in her mind. Why did she constantly compare herself—knowledge, cooking, even physical appearance—to her future DIL? Why was she more interested in making her point than in hearing from her DIL? She'd always thought of herself as self-assured and gracious. She didn't know this woman who talked loud and long in every conversation. She'd been a laid-back sort of mother. Why was she always wanting to warn her son of his future wife's weaknesses?

She had trusted God and prayed for her son's wedding. Now God had answered with a beautiful young woman. This was to be a happy occasion. Why was it that she was distressed and depressed? She felt trapped by her feelings. She asked herself, "Where is this coming from?" As she prayed, God showed her that he was asking *her* to grow. God was showing her sin, not to make her feel bad, but to make her to be more like Jesus. That's how Christian maturity happens. As God shows us our sin, we trust him to change us. On our own we naturally protect ourselves and refuse to look at our sins. But Christ holds our hand so it's not scary to look at our sin. God shines the light of his Word in our lives and we can trust him to make us more like Jesus (1 John 1:7).

Renee shared a different story. Outgoing and family-oriented, Renee suddenly realized she didn't actually know her mother-in-law. As she looked back over her fifteen years as a daughter-in-law, she asked herself how that could have happened. Renee took a hard look at herself. For years Renee had blamed her mother-in-law for the coolness in their relationship. Now she realized that she had held on to grudges until unforgiveness grew in her heart. With eyes wide open she saw that she needed to deal with her own sin. Renee wondered, *How can I make up for lost time?*

The Bible says Renee's problem is one we all share. Sin distorts our vision. The other's sin seems so big. Because of this fallen condition, we are harder on others than we are on ourselves. Jesus warned us about this painful reality, asking, "Why do you look at the splinter in your brother's eye but don't notice the beam of wood in your own eye" (Matt. 7:3)? How can we remove the splinter from our in-law's eye with a big log sticking out of our eye? Jesus is saying that if we do not repent, our own sin will hurt those we try to help. When we try to get close enough to our in-law to help her, the big log in our eye will stick into her. Jesus said we have a beam in our own eye. How can we hope to see our in-law's splinter? God's Word and his Spirit have the power, not only to take the log from your eye, but to give you new power to help others. When you deal with your own sin, God enables you to help your in-law with her splinter without hurting her.

Taking the stick out of your eye hurts. But when you repent, God brings healing. Are you God's child? Then no matter how badly your sin has hurt your relationship, trust that God is at work. He has a good purpose for you in your in-law relationship. God wants you to know more of his Son's power to overcome your sin. God uses our in-law relationships to lessen the hold our sin has on us. Don't be surprised when your in-law relationship reveals your pride, anger, envy, selfishness, and need to be right. Do you look for her weakness? Are you hard to please? Do you keep finding her faults and looking for ways to make sure she sees them? How often do you hold grudges and bring up past incidents?

You need to choose. We can cling to our own way. Or we can ask God to forgive and make us more like Jesus. If we refuse to let go of our rights, our selfish thoughts, and our insecurities—if we refuse to take our own logs out—we let the darkness blind us (1 John 2:11). Yet God stands ready to flood our lives with his light. We can pray, "Lord, I'm so ashamed. I'm your child but today I turned my back on your light and willingly walked in darkness. Please forgive me. And help me to humble myself to ask my in-law's forgiveness too." No matter how badly you have fallen, no matter how big the log in your eye, your Father always hears your cry for help. Wherever sin threatens to hurt our relationships, God also gives his children the power to love as he loves. He can restore the years the locusts have eaten (Joel 2:25). He can help you remove the log to make room for love.

Developing a God-Sized Love for Your In-Law

Think big—how would you like to change?
Do you want to:

- Be a more loving in-law?
- Wait patiently for God's work in your in-law instead of trying to make her like yourself?
- Allow the preferences of your in-law to direct your to-do list even if she doesn't appreciate your sacrifice?
- Be less self-absorbed?
- Not only work hard to restore your broken relationship because you "should," but have a heart that *wants* to do this kind of work?
- Willingly overlook the flaws of your in-law and love her in the same way you love yourself?

What's on your list? Whatever your list includes—make sure love is number one. If you think, "This will never work. You don't know my in-law. I've tried and tried—nothing I do makes any difference." Here's good news—God gives you his Spirit to do in you what you cannot do for yourself.

> For you were called to be free, brothers and sisters; only don't use this freedom as an opportunity for the flesh, but serve one another through love. For the whole law is fulfilled in one statement: Love your neighbor as yourself. But if you bite and devour one another, watch out, or you will be consumed by one another. (Gal. 5:13–15)

> But the fruit of the Spirit is love, joy, peace, patience, kindness, goodness, faithfulness, gentleness, and self-control. The law is not against such things. (Gal. 5:22–23)

The first fruit of the Spirit is love. Love for your in-law is the fruit that grows in your life by the Spirit's power working in you. Notice what this means: *You cannot produce this love on your own.* Are you relieved to hear this? If you could naturally love your in-law, love would not be a fruit of the Holy Spirit; it would be a fruit of your personality or your emotional intelligence. True love will not happen without God's Spirit working in you.

Where do you get the love for your in-law that God demands? Answer—from God. When you received Christ salvation by faith, God forgave you. He did not leave you to try and live the Christian life on your own. He filled you with his Spirit (Gal. 3:14). Love is not a matter of gritting your teeth and determining to do it. God's Spirit in you can work the miracle of love in your heart. How does love keep growing in your heart? Answer—the same way it began, by faith in God. Faith comes by hearing the Word of God (Rom. 10:17). God's Word assures us that he loves us and will give us all we need to produce the fruit of love. Even in the most difficult of in-law relationships, God fills us with his Spirit, so we keep growing in his love by faith.[4] In short, you are called to love your in-law with a God-sized love, and my friend, that's a God-sized task! Only he can do it! So let's ask him.

Ask God for love. More love for him, your husband, and your in-law. Commit to pray for your in-law. Let your life and words be filled with courtesy and grace.

Ask God for contentment in your new in-law role (Phil. 4:10–13). Your new role does not mean you've lost life's blessings. Take stock of how God continues to bless you every day. Now think again—the other woman is not a threat to you. So, add your in-law to your list of blessings! Embrace her as a companion to your entire family. Her presence opens a new phase with beautiful potential. You and your family begin a new journey with a wider horizon. Trust in the Lord and take delight in him (Ps. 37:3–6). Commit your way to him and he will give you more love, joy, and peace. And even if you aren't on the front end of this—even if you are years into the journey as an in-law—mark this season as a new beginning in your own heart. Choose to view your in-law in the ways you hope she'd view you, and trust that God really can help you be content with her as a permanent member in your life.

Ask God to help you recognize your blind spots and repent quickly of jealousy and pride. Stop comparisons. Don't view your relationship as a competition. Your in-law does not have it all. She needs your support, not your insecurity. Just like you, your in-law has problems, trials, and weaknesses. Ask God to help you learn to celebrate your in-law's joy and success. Seek to reconcile, not win.

Ask God to show you how to be generous with all he has given you. Whether it's time, money, energy, gifts, or skills, give to her freely. Not to manipulate, but to enjoy her, help her, and support her. Give of yourself to serve and be a blessing to your in-law.

God's Love

What makes some people hard to love? Imagine ways the Holy Spirit might help you to risk loving even your hard-to-love in-law. The kind of love I have always needed for all my relationships is not something that comes naturally. The kind of love we all need is God's love. God loves loving us! God showed his beautiful love to the world by sending his Son to rescue dying people. He paid the highest price for our sin—the life of his Son. Even when we did not love him, Jesus gave his life to make us God's child forever. When we receive Jesus as our Savior, the Holy Spirit puts his love into us so we can love God and others.

I once asked, "As a mom, where will I find the love I know I need to give my child?" God answered me with himself. Why not turn your heart to God? He will do the same for you. With the help of the Holy Spirit, we can love God and love our in-law as ourselves. Whatever turns our relationship with her takes, this kind of love really is possible. Remember that love is like fruit that grows in your heart. Through obedience to God and reliance on his power, whether rain or shine, your love for your in-law will get sweeter and sweeter. ✐

Discussion Questions

1. In this chapter, we outlined all the things love is, according to 1 Corinthians 13:4–7. Which of these seems most difficult for you to display to your in-law? Why?

2. How might 1 Corinthians 13:4–7 guide the content of your prayers?

3. When God accomplishes what only he can do, he alone gets the glory. What circumstance do you face in your in-law relationship that you are unable to solve?

4. One culprit behind a lack of love toward our in-law is having a log in our own eye. What log in your eye might need removing?

5. What are some ways your lack of love may be hurting your in-law?

6. In what situations have you been trusting in your own strength to produce biblical love for your in-law (or anyone else)?

7. On the flip side, think back over the relationship with your in-law. How have you seen God provide what you need to love your in-law as God loves you? How might that memory strengthen your faith in this season?

NOTES

Chapter 1: First Impressions

1. Elizabeth Graham, *Mothers-in-Law vs. Daughters-in-Law* (Kansas City: Beacon Hill Press, 2010), 26–29.

Chapter 2: Biblical Hope for the Relationship

1. *ESV Gospel Transformation Bible* (Carol Stream, IL: Crossway, 2011), 336.
2. Paul Miller, *A Loving Life: In a World of Broken Relationships* (Carol Stream, IL: Crossway, 2014), 22–23.
3. Miller, 75.
4. *ESV Gospel Transformation Bible*, 336.
5. Miller, *A Loving Life*, 24–34.
6. Miller, 35–52.
7. Miller, 130–38.
8. Miller, 151–54.

Chapter 3: Leave and Cleave

1. Deb DeArmond, *Related by Chance, Family by Choice* (Grand Rapids: Kregel, 2013), 63.
2. *NIV Zondervan Study Bible* (Grand Rapids: Zondervan, 2015), 2409.
3. Paul Tripp, "What Does It Mean to Be One Flesh?" *www .paultripp.com*, February 19, 2019, https://www.paultripp.com/ask -paul-tripp/posts/what-does-it-mean-to-be-one-flesh.

4. John Piper, "Can I Leave and Cleave If I Live with My Parents," *Ask Pastor John*, December 8, 2017, https://www.desiringgod.org/interviews/can-i-leave-and-cleave-if-we-live-with-my-parents.

5. Dave Harvey, "6 Surprises Every Premarital Counselor Should Cover," *The Gospel Coalition*, June 29, 2017, https://www.thegospelcoalition.org/article/6-surprises-every-premarital-counselor-should-cover/.

6. Deb DeArmond, *Related by Chance, Family by Choice* (Grand Rapids: Kregel, 2013), 62.

Chapter 4: Expectations

1. Paul David Tripp, *Lost in the Middle: Midlife and the Grace of God* (Wapwallopen, PA: Shepherd Press, 2004).

2. This phrase has become common proverbial wisdom in many circles, and takes many forms, but many people trace it back to Alexander Pope.

3. Deb DeArmond, *Related by Chance, Family by Choice* (Grand Rapids: Kregel, 2013) 95–97.

Chapter 5: Communicating Well

1. Marshall Segal, "People-Pleasing That Pleases God," *Desiring God*, December 20, 2020, https://www.desiringgod.org/articles/people-pleasing-that-pleases-god.

2. *Merriam-Webster*, s.v. "communion," accessed January 20, 2021, https://www.merriam-webster.com/dictionary/communion.

3. Nancy Wilson, "17: Flexibility," *Femina*, September 11, 2020, https://podcasts.apple.com/ie/podcast/femina/id1513264253.

4. Andrea Polard, "In-Law Blues No More," *Psychology Today*, March 31, 2019, https://www.psychologytoday.com/us/blog/unified-theory-happiness/201903/in-law-blues-no-more.

5. Juli Slattery, "Java with Juli: Love Your Husband By Loving Your Mother-In-Law," Focus on the Family, June 22, 2017,

https://www.focusonthefamily.com/marriage/java-with-juli-love
-your-husband-by-loving-your-mother-in-law/.

6. Jani Ortland, "The Other Woman in His Life," *Desiring God*, January 9, 2020, https://www.desiringgod.org/articles/the
-other-woman-in-his-life.

7. Yvonne Fulbright, "Have In-Law Issues?" *Psychology Today*, October 14, 2013, https://www.psychologytoday.com/us/blog
/mate-relate-and-communicate/201310/have-in-law-issues.

8. Jen Oshman, "Best Pre-Marital Advice We Got and Love to Give" *jenoshman.com*, February 26, 2019, https://www.jenoshman
.com/jen-oshman-blog/2019/2/26/best-pre-marital-advice-we-got
-and-love-to-give?rq=marriage%20.

Chapter 6: Conflict

1. Ken Sande, *The Peacemaker: A Biblical Guide to Resolving Personal Conflict* (Grand Rapids: Baker, 2006), 109.

2. We'd like to give as much credit as possible to Ken Sande and his book *The Peacemaker* for our advice in this chapter. His expertise is invaluable, and much of what we relay in this chapter is due to our internalization of his work. We've cited him clearly when using a direct quotation, but we'd also like to make it clear that we are approaching this chapter according to his general perspective on conflict, and much of what we share stems from the wisdom we've gleaned from him over the years.

3. Sande, *The Peacemaker*, 31.

4. Again, we are indebted to Ken Sande's perspective on conflict, as well as typical responses to it, in his book, *The Peacemaker*.

5. Danielle Sallade, "The Way to Have a Good Fight," *The Gospel Coalition Podcast*, September 13, 2019, https://www.the
gospelcoalition.org/podcasts/tgc-podcast/way-good-fight/.

6. These practical steps stem from a compilation of sources—our own study of Scripture, *The Peacemaker* by Ken Sande, and *Christ-Centered Conflict Resolution* by Tony Merida.

7. Alexander Strauch, *If You Bite and Devour One Another* (Colorado Springs: Lewis & Roth, 2011), 87.

8. Gaye Clark, "When Your Reconciliation Doesn't Reconcile," The Gospel Coalition, December 26, 2017, https://www.thegospel coalition.org/article/when-reconciliation-doesnt-reconcile/.

Chapter 7: A New Generation

1. Sue Edwards and Barbara Neumann, *Organic Mentoring: A Mentor's Guide to Relationships with Next Generation Women* (Grand Rapids: Kregel Publications, 2014), 31–53.

2. Edwards and Newmann, 31–53.

3. *ESV Gospel Transformation Study Bible: Christ in All of Scripture, Grace for All of Life,* 2019; https://www.google.com/books/edition /ESV_Gospel_Transformation_Study_Bible_Ch/C5-fDwAAQBAJ ?hl=en&gbpv=1&dq=with+no+sense+of+envy,+rivalry,+superiority +or+inferiority,+because+this+is+the+kind+of+love+sharing+amo ng+Father,+Son,+and+Spirit.%E2%80%9D&pg=PT3921&printsec =frontcover.

4. Marshall Segal, "People-Pleasing That Pleases God," *Desiring God,* December 20, 2020, https://www.desiringgod.org/articles /people-pleasing-that-pleases-god.

5. Sue Edwards and Barbara Neumann, *Organic Mentoring: A Mentor's Guide to Relationships with Next Generation Women* (Grand Rapids: Kregel Publications, 2014), 98–105.

6. Jani Ortland, "The Other Woman in His Life," *Desiring God,* January 9, 2020, https://www.desiringgod.org/articles/the -other-woman-in-his-life.

Chapter 8: Faithful Expressions

1. Thomas Schreiner, "Don't Judge or Despise One Another—Romans 14:1–12 (MP3)," Monergism, https://audio.clifton baptist.org/audio/2012/2012-12-30_Dont_Judge_or_Despise_One_Another_Rom_14.1-12_Tom_Schreiner.mp3.

Chapter 9: Suffering Together

1. Elisabeth Elliot, *Keep a Quiet Heart* (Grand Rapids: Revell, 1995).

2. Stacy Reaoch, "God Fills Our Lives with Trials," *Desiring God*, September 7, 2016, https://www.desiringgod.org/articles /god-fills-our-lives-with-trials.

3. Ed Welch, *Caring for One Another: 8 Ways to Cultivate Meaningful Relationships* (Wheaton, IL: Crossway, 2018), 45.

4. Dave Furman, *Being There: How to Love Those Who Are Hurting* (Wheaton, Crossway, 2016), 38.

Chapter 10: Going Forward in Love

1. V. D. Verbrugge, 1 Corinthians, in T. Longman III and David E. Garland, David E. eds., *The Expositor's Bible Commentary: Romans–Galatians Revised Edition-Vol. 11* (Grand Rapids: Zondervan, 2008), 372.

2. Gotquestions.org. "What Does It Mean That Love Does Not Boast?" https://www.gotquestions.org/love-does-not-boast.html.

3. John Piper, "What Love Does and Does Not Do," *Desiring God*, January 3, 2007, https://www.desiringgod.org/articles/what -love-does-and-does-not-do.

4. Piper, "What Love Does and Does Not Do."